D1134478

UNFORGETTABLE
SENIOR JOKES

Also published by Michael O'Mara Books:

The Little Book of Senior Jokes by Geoff Tibballs

Are You Turning Into Your Dad? by Joseph Piercy

A Dyslexic Walks into a Bra: The ultimate compendium of the best jokes, gags and one-liners by Nick Harris

UNFORGETTABLE
SENIOR JOKES

Geoff Tibballs

MICHAEL O'MARA BOOKS

First published in Great Britain in 2011 by
Michael O'Mara Books Limited
9 Lion Yard
Tremadoc Road
London SW4 7NQ

A CIP catalogue record for this book is available from the British Library.

Papers used by Michael O'Mara Books Limited are natural, recyclable products made from wood grown in sustainable forests. The manufacturing processes conform to the environmental regulations of the country of origin.

ISBN: 978-1-84317-694-7 in hardback print format

1 2 3 4 5 6 7 8 9 10

Cover design by Marc Burville-Riley

Designed and typeset by Design 23

Printed and bound in Great Britain by Clays Ltd, St Ives plc

www.mombooks.com

INTRODUCTION

When the publishers asked me if I wanted to compile another book of senior jokes, my immediate reaction was: 'Another? Why, did I write one before?' You see, that's what happens when you hit a certain age. Three things occur: the first is your memory goes, and I can't remember the other two.

The veteran American comedian Red Buttons once defined old age as being when your wife says, 'Let's go upstairs and make love', and you answer, 'Sorry, honey, I can't do both.' Jokes about the shortcomings of senior citizens are as old as the hills, and more often than not seniors themselves are the ones who tell them – because along with experience, wisdom and a missionary-like zeal for Werther's Originals comes the priceless gift of being able to laugh at ourselves. Sometimes it's the only thing that keeps us sane in a world where a penny for some people's thoughts is still a fair price.

So don't listen to kids who try to write us off as a bunch of boring old fogeys. Just because after painting the town red we now have to take a long rest before applying the second coat and our idea of a good party is one that gets us home in time for the ten o'clock news, it doesn't mean we don't still know how to enjoy ourselves. In fact many stand-up comedians prefer an audience of seniors. Not only are we often less inhibited than the young but with our lousy memories every joke seems new!

The Funeral Procession

A funeral procession made its way solemnly down the road. Six close members of the family were carrying the coffin between them. On top of the coffin was a fishing line, a net and some bait.

A passer-by remarked: 'He must have been a very keen fisherman.'

'Oh, he still is,' said another. 'As a matter of fact he's off to the river as soon as they've buried his wife.'

An Old Relic

An elderly museum guide was answering questions from tourists about the various exhibits.

Studying a display of fossils, one tourist asked: 'How old is this fossil?'

'Fifty million and four years old,' replied the guide.

'That's incredible,' said the tourist. 'How can you be so precise about the age?'

'Well,' explained the guide, 'when I started this job I was told the fossil was fifty million years old – and that was four years ago.'

A Hard Lesson

Old friends Bert and Jim were eighty and eighty-six respectively. They met one morning in their local library, Bert travelling by bus but Jim preferring to jog there, as he did most mornings. When Jim arrived he wasn't even out of breath, prompting Bert to ask how he had so much stamina at his age.

Jim revealed: 'I eat rye bread every day. It's a well-known fact that it keeps your energy levels high, and gives you great stamina with the ladies. Trust me, you'll never be short of female admirers.'

Impressed by these claims, Bert stopped off at the bakery on the way home. As he was looking around, the female sales assistant asked him if he needed any assistance.

'Do you have any rye bread?' he asked.

'Yes,' she said. 'There's a whole shelf of it. Would you like some?'

'Yes. I'd like five loaves, please,' he said.

'My goodness!' she exclaimed. 'Five loaves! By the time you get to the fifth loaf, it'll be hard.'

'I can't believe it!' cried Bert. 'Everyone knows about this stuff except me!'

That Sinking Feeling

Two elderly women were in a beauty parlour getting their hair done when in walked a twenty-one-year-old girl with a low-cut blouse that revealed the tattoo of a rose on one breast. One woman leaned over to the other and whispered: 'Poor thing. She doesn't know it, but in fifty years she'll have a long-stemmed rose in a hanging basket!'

Incontinence Helpline

An old man phoned the incontinence helpline and told the adviser: 'I have a problem with incontinence. Before I go into details, is all the information I give you confidential?'

'Of course,' said the adviser. 'Now, where are you ringing from?'

'The waist down,' replied the old man.

Lassie Come Home

An elderly farmer was upset because his faithful sheepdog had been missing for over two weeks. His wife suggested: 'Why don't you put an ad in the paper to get him back?'

'That's a good idea,' said the farmer. 'I'll do that.' So he placed the ad in the paper, but a month later there was still no sign of the sheepdog.

The farmer's wife said: 'I really thought that ad would work. What did you write in it?'

The farmer replied: '"Here, boy."'

Lost Track

Three old men were chatting at a train station. They were so engrossed in their conversation that they didn't hear the guard blow his whistle to signal the train's departure. In the ensuing confusion two of them managed to scramble aboard the train as it pulled away, but the third didn't make it.

The guard came over to console him. 'Don't worry,' said the guard. 'Two of you made it, and there's another train in an hour.'

'No, you don't understand,' said the old man. 'They came to see me off!'

It's the Thought That Counts

Two married men were drinking in a bar. One said to the other: 'I got my wife a bag and a belt for her fiftieth birthday.'

'Oh, really?' said the other. 'That was very thoughtful of you.'

'Well, she wasn't very pleased,' said the first, 'but the Hoover works fine now.'

Burning Desire

An old man phoned the fire department and said: 'I have just had my front yard landscaped. I have beautiful new flower beds, a rose border, a new fish pond and a fountain.'

'That sounds very nice,' said the fire chief, 'but what does that have to do with the fire service?'

The caller said: 'Because next door's house is on fire, and I don't want your men trampling all over my front yard!'

Medicine Man

An elderly man went to the doctor and said: 'It's been a month since I last came to see you, doc, but I can't say I'm feeling any better.'

'I see,' said the doctor. 'And did you follow the instructions on the medicine I gave you?'

'I sure did,' he replied. 'The bottle said: "Keep tightly closed."'

Keep Your Hair On!

A woman visited the undertaker's to arrange her late husband's funeral.

'Have you any special requests as to how you would like your husband dressed?' asked the undertaker.

'Well,' said his widow, 'he was bald and never went anywhere without his wig but every time I put it on his head, it just slides off.'

'No problem,' said the undertaker reassuringly. 'I'll sort that out for you. Come back in an hour and a half.'

Ninety minutes later she returned and, as promised, the wig was perfectly placed on the dead man's head.

'Oh, thank you so much,' she said. 'Now, you must let me pay you something for your trouble – and I won't take no for an answer.'

'Very well, if you insist,' said the undertaker. 'Just give me two dollars for the nails.'

Showing Her Age

Two women friends met up for coffee one morning. One said: 'Be honest. Do you think my skin is starting to show its age?'

'I can't tell,' said the other. 'There are too many wrinkles.'

Invisible Wrinkles

A woman went into hospital to have her wrinkles removed, but she woke up to find that the surgeon had given her breast implants.

'What on earth have you done?' she demanded. 'I came in here to have the wrinkles on my face removed, but instead you've given me these huge breasts.'

'Yes,' said the surgeon, 'but at least nobody's looking at your wrinkles any more.'

A Telltale Sign

A senior man was crossing the road when he was hit by a car, which then sped off without stopping. A police officer arrived on the scene and asked the injured man: 'Did you get a look at the driver?'

'No,' he said, 'but I can tell you for certain that it was my ex-wife.'

'How do you know that?' asked the officer.

'Easy,' said the man. 'I'd recognize her laugh anywhere.'

Piece of String

Old friends Harry and George had been drinking in a bar for most of Tuesday. At ten o'clock in the evening, George was ready to leave but Harry said: 'I daren't go home. See this piece of string around my finger? Well, before I set off this lunchtime, my wife asked me to do something and to make sure I wouldn't forget she tied this piece of string around my finger. But now I can't remember what it was I'm supposed to do, so I'm afraid to face her.'

A few days later the two men met up again. 'So,' said George, 'did you remember what the string was for?'

'Oh, don't ask!' exclaimed Harry. 'I was so worried

about it that I didn't dare go home until Wednesday evening. Sure enough, my wife gave me hell.'

'And did she tell you what the string was for?'

'Yes she did,' sighed Harry. 'It had been to remind me to make sure I went home early!'

Home Repairs

After thirty years of marriage, the honeymoon was well and truly over. One day the wife told her husband that the vacuum cleaner was broken and ordered him to fix it.

'Do I look like the Hoover repairman?' he asked indignantly, and continued watching TV.

The next day she informed him that the washing machine had broken and told him to fix it.

'Do I look like the Zanussi repairman?' he barked, and continued watching TV.

The day after that she told him that the computer was broken and ordered him to fix it.

'Do I look like the Dell repairman?' he growled, and continued watching TV.

A few weeks later the husband said: 'I see you managed to get everything fixed. How did you get it all done so cheap?'

'Well,' said the wife, 'Michael next door agreed to do the repairs for free if I'd sleep with him or sing him a song.'

'What song did you sing?' asked the husband.

The wife snapped: 'Do I look like Tina Turner?'

A Creative Dish

A woman was so happy playing bridge with friends at a neighbour's house one afternoon that she lost track of the time. When she realized it was almost five o'clock, she grabbed her coat and said: 'I must go now. My husband will be home in half an hour and there'll be hell to pay if his dinner isn't ready.'

To her horror, she found that all she had in the cupboard was a lettuce leaf, an egg, and a can of cat food. In a panic, she opened the can of cat food, stirred in the egg, and garnished it with the lettuce leaf just as she heard her husband's car pull up outside. She greeted him lovingly and then watched in apprehension as he sat down to the improvised meal.

Against all odds, he really enjoyed it. 'Darling, this is the best dinner you've made me in ages!' he enthused. 'Just right for a summer's day. We must have it again!' Naturally she kept quiet about the ingredients.

So on every subsequent bridge afternoon, she made him the same dish of lettuce, egg and cat food. She told her bridge friends about it and they were all horrified. 'If you're not careful, you'll kill him!' they warned.

Then six weeks later, her husband died.

At the next bridge gathering, one of the women exploded with rage. 'I said you'd end up killing him,' she told the wife, 'feeding the poor man cat food every week!'

'I didn't kill him,' the wife protested. 'He fell off the window ledge while he was licking himself.'

Hot Bath

Feeling stressed out while working from home one day, a man decided to take a long hot bath, but just as he had made himself comfortable, the front doorbell rang. The man climbed out of the tub, wrapped a large towel around his waist, wrapped his head in a small towel, put on his slippers, and went to the door. It was a salesman trying to sell him a new conservatory. The salesman was sent packing and after slamming the door, the man returned to his hot bath.

No sooner had he climbed back in than there was

another ring at the doorbell. The man climbed out of the tub, wrapped a large towel around his waist, wrapped his head in a smaller towel, put on his slippers, and trudged downstairs to answer the door. It was an energy company trying to persuade him to change his power supplier. Slamming the door, the man returned to his hot bath.

Five minutes later, the doorbell rang again. On went the slippers and towels as before, but as he tottered towards the bathroom door, he slipped on a wet patch of floor and hurt his back in falling against the hard porcelain of the tub. Cursing silently, he struggled into his street clothes and, with every movement causing a sharp, stabbing pain, he drove to the doctor's surgery.

After examining him thoroughly, the doctor said: 'You've been lucky. There are no bones broken. But you need to relax. Why don't you go home and take a long hot bath?'

Touchy Topic

A sturdy woman in her sixties queued at the drugstore for over fifteen minutes. Eventually the girl behind the counter served her and said: 'I'm really sorry about your wait.'

The woman snapped back: 'Well, you're not exactly skinny yourself!'

Dating Agency

A scruffy man in his sixties who had been single all his life joined a dating agency but none of the dates he went on worked out. Disenchanted, he went back to the agency and said to the proprietor: 'Have you got someone on your books who doesn't care what I look like, isn't concerned about my personal hygiene and has a big pair of boobs?'

The proprietor checked the computer database and said: 'Actually we do have one. But it's you.'

Choppy Waters

A cruise ship crossing the Atlantic encountered rough seas. A young woman was undressing in her cabin when she suddenly felt seasick. In a panic she rushed into the corridor and headed for the bathroom, but it wasn't until she collided with an elderly gentleman that she realized she was completely naked.

Instinctively she let out a scream. The old man, who was also suffering from chronic seasickness, looked at her sadly and said: 'Don't worry about it, miss. I don't think I'll live to tell anyone.'

Innocent Explanation

A woman was fretting because her husband was late home from work one evening. 'I'm sure he's having an affair,' she said to her elderly mother.

'Why do you always think the worst?' asked the mother. 'Maybe he's just been in a car crash.'

Nag, Nag, Nag

After being married for over thirty years, a wife slapped her husband around the face after discovering a piece of paper in his jacket pocket with the name 'Mary-Lou' written on it.

'Why did you do that?' he protested. 'It was just the name of a horse I bet on yesterday.'

The following day she slapped him again.

'What was that for?' he wailed.

'Your horse called last night.'

Mother's Pride

Old Mrs Finkelstein was so proud. 'Did you hear about my son Bernie?' she said to her neighbour. 'He's going to see a psychiatrist twice a week.'

'Is that good?' queried the neighbour.

'Good?!' exclaimed Mrs Finkelstein. 'Of course it's good. Not only is he paying top dollar but all he talks about for the hour is me!'

Marriage Guidance

Tony had been married for thirty-seven years but one day he moaned to his friend Ted that all the excitement had gone out of his marriage.

'That often happens when people have been married for a long time,' said Ted. 'Have you ever thought about having an affair? That might put a bit of zest back into your relationship.'

'No, no, I couldn't possibly do that,' said Tony. 'It wouldn't be right.'

'Get real,' said Ted. 'We're living in the twenty-first century. These things happen all the time.'

'But what if my wife found out?' asked Tony.

'No problem. Be upfront. Tell her about it in advance.'

Tony gave the idea some thought and eventually came round to Ted's way of thinking. So he plucked up the courage to break the news to his wife the next morning while she was reading a magazine over breakfast.

'Honey,' he began hesitantly, 'I don't want you to take this the wrong way…and please remember that I'm only doing this because I truly, truly love you, otherwise I would never dream of it…but I think maybe…just possibly… having an affair might bring us closer together.'

'Forget it,' said his wife, without even looking up from her magazine. 'I've tried it, and it's never worked.'

Death on the Course

Peter received a call from the coroner who wanted to talk about his wife's recent death. Peter told him the sad story: 'We were out playing golf at our local course, as we usually did on a Wednesday afternoon because the rates then are cheaper for seniors. Anyway we were on the eighth hole, and Beatrice, my wife, was standing on the ladies' tee about thirty yards ahead of the men's tee when I hit my drive. From the sound when the ball hit her head and the way she dropped like a stone, I knew instantly that she was dead. God knows where the ball ended up!'

'I see,' said the coroner. 'Well, that explains the injury to her head but what about the ball that was wedged up her back passage?'

'Oh, that,' sighed Peter. 'That was my provisional.'

Long Wait

Two old ladies were sitting waiting for a bus. One said: 'I hate it when the buses run late. I've been sitting here so long that my butt has fallen asleep.'

'I know,' said the other. 'I heard it snoring.'

Dream Woman

Bill and George were enjoying their regular Thursday night drink in the pub when the topic of conversation turned to dreams. 'Last night I dreamed I was fishing in Canada,' said Bill. 'It was just me and my fishing rod and this big beautiful lake. What a dream!' 'I had a great dream, too,' said George. 'I dreamed I was on a date with two gorgeous young women and having the time of my life.' 'Hey!' cried Bill, pretending to be hurt. 'You dreamed you were with two gorgeous young women and you didn't call me?' 'I did,' said George. 'But your wife said you'd gone fishing.'

Gas Attack

An elderly man went to the doctor and said: 'Doctor, I suffer from the most embarrassing complaint. I get terrible gas. It happens whenever I bend over.'

'Very well,' said the doctor. 'I'd like you to stand up for me, please, and bend over that chair.'

The old man duly bent over and as he did so, he let out a loud noise, accompanied by the most awful stench.

'I see,' said the doctor. He then reached for a long pole that was propped against the wall and said: 'Right, this should do the trick.'

The old man looked petrified. 'What are you going to do with that?' he asked.

The doctor replied: 'I'm going to open the window to let some air into this room.'

Beauty Treatment

A teenage boy watched in fascination as his mother gently rubbed cold cream on her face.

'Why are you rubbing cold cream on your face?' he asked eventually.

'To make myself look beautiful,' replied his mother.

A few minutes later she began removing the cream with a tissue.

'What's the matter?' asked her son. 'Giving up?'

Auntie Climax

A couple's marriage nearly broke up because of the presence in their household of old Auntie Ethel. She lived with them for twenty long years, always bad-tempered, always demanding. She made their lives hell. Then finally she passed away.

On the way back from the cemetery, the husband confessed to his wife: 'Darling, if I didn't love you so much I don't think I could have put up with having your Auntie Ethel in the house all those years.'

His wife looked at him aghast. 'My Auntie Ethel?' she cried. 'I thought she was *your* Auntie Ethel!'

Anniversary Gift

As they prepared to celebrate their thirtieth wedding anniversary, a husband asked his wife: 'What would you like as an anniversary present? How about a new winter coat – designer label, of course?'

'No, I don't think so,' replied the wife.

'What about a new car for you to run about in?'

'No, I don't think so,' said the wife.

'What about that diamond ring you saw in the jeweller's?'

'No, I don't think so,' repeated the wife. 'You see, what I really want is a divorce.'

'A divorce?' said the husband. 'Sorry, darling, I wasn't intending to spend that much!'

Tourist Trap

An Australian aborigine was fishing when a crocodile suddenly leaped from the water and grabbed him by the legs. The crocodile was partway through devouring the man when a boatload of senior American tourists passed by.

One woman remarked loudly: 'I thought aborigines

were meant to be poor. Well, there's one over there with a Lacoste sleeping bag!'

The Power of Hypnotism

A senior woman came home and told her husband: 'You know the headaches I've been getting for years? Well, they've finally gone.'

'That's great news,' he said. 'How did you get rid of them?

She said: 'I went to see a hypnotist and he told me to stand in front of a mirror, stare at myself and repeat over and over: "I do not have a headache, I do not have a headache, I do not have a headache." And it worked! The headaches are all gone.'

'Well, that's wonderful,' said the husband.

She went on: 'I don't like to say it but you haven't exactly been a ball of fire in the bedroom department these last few years. Why don't you go and see the hypnotist to find out if he can do anything for that?'

Reluctantly the husband agreed to try it.

After his first appointment with the hypnotist, the husband returned home, ripped off his clothes, led his wife into the bedroom, threw her on to the bed and said:

'Don't move. I'll be right back.'

He went into the bathroom and emerged a few minutes later. He then made passionate love to his wife, the best sex they'd had in years.

'Wow! That was wonderful,' she said.

The husband said: 'Don't move. I'll be right back.'

He went back into the bathroom and when he came out he made love to her again, this time even better than before.

'Oh, my God! That was amazing,' she sighed ecstatically.

Again he said: 'Don't move. I'll be right back.'

He returned to the bathroom, but this time she quietly followed him. Peering through the partly open door, she saw him standing in front of the mirror, staring at himself and repeating over and over: 'She is not my wife, she is not my wife, she is not my wife.'

Something Missing

While sitting at a bar, a customer noticed an old man slumped over a table, evidently having had too much to drink. The bartender asked the customer whether he would mind driving the old man home and gave him his address.

The customer went over and tried to wake the old man but received no response. He then helped him to his feet but the old man fell to the floor in a heap. The customer wondered how anyone could drink that much.

Taking the old man by the arm, the customer dragged him out to the car. Once there, he leaned him against the side of the car while he searched for the keys but the old man slid to the ground. He eventually found his keys, piled the old the man into the car and drove him to the address the bartender had given him. He opened the passenger door but the old man just crumpled to the ground. Cursing under his breath, the customer dragged him to the front door of the house. He let go of him to knock on the door, whereupon the old man immediately fell down again. He picked him back up just as the old man's wife answered the door.

'Mrs Davies?' said the customer. 'I'm afraid your husband has had a little too much to drink tonight, so I drove him home.'

'That's very kind of you,' said the wife, 'but where's his wheelchair?'

Charity Drive

Two middle-aged women bumped into each other in the supermarket. 'How's your husband?' asked one. 'Somebody told me he tried to kill himself. Is it true?'

'I'm afraid so,' said the other. 'It's been terrible, it really has. You see, he got in debt and owed £2,000 to a loan shark. He was scared we were going to lose everything. He was so upset that last month he drove to the edge of a cliff and parked there, his head resting on the steering wheel. But all the nice people there had a whip-round and they got him his £2,000. I tell you, it was a good job his bus was full that day.'

Acting Single

A wife wanted to do something special for her husband's birthday, so she told him: 'Even though we've been married for twenty-eight years, because it's your birthday, you can go out on the town tonight with your friends and pretend that we're not married yet.'

'No thanks,' he said. 'I don't want to think I've got twenty-eight years of this ahead of me!'

Remembering the Seventies

Ellen and Ruth were reminiscing about 1970s fashions. 'I had an Afghan coat,' said Ellen, 'and a cheesecloth shirt.'
'Did you have hot pants?' asked Ruth.
'I still do,' said Ellen. 'But that's the menopause for you.'

Death Wish

On her death bed an old woman asked her husband:
'How many cars have you ordered to go to the cemetery?'
    'Four,' he replied.
    'Does that include the hearse?'
    'Yes.'
    'Four is too many. Cancel one.'
    'Whatever you say, darling.'
    'And I want you to promise me something else.'
    'Anything, darling.'
    'I want you to travel in the same car as my sister.'
    'But you know we haven't spoken to each other for over twenty years.'
    'I know, but it's what I want. Promise me you'll do it.'
    'Very well,' the husband sighed. 'I'll do it. But I'll tell you now, it will ruin the day for me.'

The Wrong Game

A man with middle-aged spread had tried all kinds of exercise in an attempt to slim down. He joined a gym, he took up swimming, he went for early morning runs but nothing reduced his bulging waistline. As a last resort, his doctor suggested that he take up golf. So the man went and out bought a set of golf clubs, but a few weeks later he was back at the doctor's requesting to take up some other sport.

'Why? What's wrong with golf?' asked the doctor. 'It's a wonderful game.'

'Well,' explained the patient, indicating his outsize stomach, 'the trouble is that when I put the ball where I can see it, I can't hit it. And when I put it where I can hit it, I can't see it!'

Virgin Fliers

Back in the 1940s, an elderly couple who had never flown before took a plane from New York to Los Angeles. When they made their first stop – at Philadelphia – a red truck arrived to put fuel in the aeroplane.

A little while later they landed in Pittsburgh, and again a red truck pulled up to fill the plane's tanks with fuel.

Each time they landed to discharge or take on passengers, a red truck would pull up and add fuel to the tanks. Finally, after landing in Kansas City and seeing the truck pull up again, the husband turned to his wife and said: 'We sure are making good time.'

'Yes, we are,' agreed his wife, 'and so is that red truck!'

A Night on the Town

Trying to put the life back into their marriage, a wife said to her husband: 'Darling, let's go out tonight and have some fun.'

'I suppose we could,' he replied, 'but if you get home before me, leave the hallway light on.'

Burial Plot

Struggling to think what to get his elderly mother-in-law for her birthday, a man eventually decided to buy her a large burial plot in an exclusive cemetery. He thought it was a novel and practical gift, but the following year he was stuck for ideas, so he didn't buy her anything.

'Why haven't you bought me a present this year?' she complained.

'I don't know what you're moaning about,' he said. 'You still haven't used the present I got you last year.'

Hopping Mad

A small boy said to his grandfather: 'Make a frog noise for me, Grandpa.'

'No, son, I don't really feel like making a frog noise right now.'

'Oh, please, please, Grandpa, make a frog noise.'

'Why are you so keen for me to make a frog noise?'

'Because Dad says when you croak we can go to Disneyland.'

Skinny Dipping

One hot summer afternoon, a pretty young woman came across a secluded pool, largely hidden from view by a row of bushes. After checking that nobody was around, she took off all her clothes, but just as she was about to jump in, an old farmer appeared from behind the bushes.

'I've been watching you!' he yelled. 'This is private farm land, and I'm the owner. Swimming in this pool is strictly prohibited.'

'You could have told me that before I undressed!' she cried.

The old farmer replied with a smile: 'Swimming is prohibited; undressing isn't.'

The Unluckiest Man

Jim was the world's unluckiest man. He had a genuine enthusiasm for life, but at every turn he was beset by misfortune. He loved poker, but poker did not love him. He played the stock market, but always sold at the wrong time. He invested heavily in property, but always just as the market crashed. His first three wives left him for close friends of his.

Through all of this, the one constant in his life was golf. He wasn't much of a player – only occasionally did he break 100 – but come rain or shine, he was out there every weekend. Then one day he was taken ill and died. In accordance with his wishes, he was cremated and his ashes were to be scattered just off the fairway on the eleventh hole of his local course.

A small gathering of friends turned up at the eleventh to witness the ceremony. It was a beautiful sunny day but then just as the ashes were being strewn, a sudden gust of wind sprang up and blew Jim out of bounds.

Treated with Respect

A Greek family came to visit their elderly father in a nursing home. 'How is it in here?' they asked. 'Are they taking good care of you, because we weren't sure if it was the right place for you?'

'It's wonderful,' replied the father. 'Everyone is so respectful and courteous. Let me tell you how well they treat the residents. There's a musician in here, he's eighty-five years old and he hasn't played the violin in twenty years, but they still call him "Maestro". There's a judge in here, he's ninety years old and he hasn't sat on the bench for twenty-five years, but everyone still calls him "Your Honour". And me, I haven't had sex for thirty years, but they still call me "The F***ing Greek!"'

Double Life

A middle-aged man was drowning his sorrows in a bar with a fellow drinker. 'I had everything,' he groaned. 'Two kids, a house in the country and the love of a beautiful woman. Then suddenly it was all gone.'
'What happened?' asked his drinking partner.
'My wife found out.'

The New Toy

Having just bought a toaster oven, an elderly woman was keen to try it out. However she was forgetful and instead of watching it closely, she wandered off to another room. Within seconds, smoke began billowing from the toaster.

'Quick!' yelled her husband. 'Get the owner's manual!'

She hurried back into the kitchen. 'I can't find it anywhere,' she cried. 'Ooops…!'

'What is it?' asked her husband.

'Well,' she said resignedly, 'the toast is fine but the owner's manual is burned to a crisp.'

Annual Physical

A man in his eighties went to the doctor for his annual health check-up. He told the doctor: 'I'm getting really forgetful. I forget where I live, I forget where I've parked my car, and I go into shops and I can't remember what it is that I want. And when I do get to the checkout, I find I've forgotten my wallet. It's getting pretty bad, doc. What can I do?'

The doctor thought for a moment and said: 'Pay me in advance.'

The Curse of the Call Centre

A little old lady tried to phone her local bank but was put through instead to the bank's call centre in India.

'Is that the High Street branch?' she asked.

'No, madam,' replied the voice at the other end. 'It is now company policy to deal with telephone calls centrally.'

'Well, I really need to speak to the branch,' said the old lady.

'Madam, if you just let me know your query, I'm sure I can help you.'

'I don't think you can, young man. I need to speak to the branch.'

The call centre operator was adamant. 'There's nothing that the branch can help you with that can't be dealt with by me.'

'Very well then,' sighed the old lady. 'Can you just check on the counter? Did I leave my gloves behind when I came in this morning?'

Constipation Cure

A man in his seventies went to see a doctor for advice on how to deal with his terrible constipation. The doctor questioned him about his diet, and the man admitted that the only vegetable he ever ate was peas.

'That's almost certainly the cause of your constipation,' said the doctor. 'All those peas you've been eating for years have clogged up your system. I'm afraid you'll have to give them up for good.'

A few years later, the old man was sitting in the lounge of a retirement home chatting to two of the female residents. 'If there's one thing I miss in life,' said one of the women, 'it's a nice piece of cheese. But I had to give it up for health reasons.'

The other woman said: 'It's the same with me and milk. I'd love a glass of milk, but the doctor has warned me not to.'

'I know how you feel,' said the old man. 'I haven't had a pea for seven years.'

The two women immediately jumped to their feet and screamed: 'Right, anyone who can't swim, grab a table!'

Seniors' Prank

A teenage boy was swaggering down the street when he heard voices chanting from behind a high wooden fence: 'Eighteen, eighteen, eighteen…'

Curious to find out what was going on, he tried to look over the fence but wasn't tall enough. Then he spotted a knot in the wood so he put his eye to the hole. He just managed to spy a group of old people sitting in deckchairs and chanting before a finger came out of nowhere and poked him in the eye.

As he staggered back, the old people started chanting: 'Nineteen, nineteen, nineteen…'

Voices of the Dead

Mrs Kaminski was a regular visitor to Madame Olga's séance parlour and for months had been trying to persuade her husband Jerzy to accompany her.

'Jerzy, she's a real gypsy and she brings the voices of the dead into our world. We all talk to them. Last week, I spoke with my mother. For a modest fee you can talk to your dear departed grandmother.'

So Jerzy agreed to go along to Madame Olga's next

séance. He sat at a table, holding hands with the person on either side. They all made a low humming noise while Madame Olga, lost in a trance, caressed a crystal ball.

After a few minutes, Madame Olga called out: 'I am in contact with the dead! It is a woman, an old woman… I'm getting a name…She says she is Mr Kaminski's grandmother.'

'Elka?' said Jerzy, overcome with emotion.

'Ah, Jerzy,' replied a thin, shaky voice. 'It is good to speak to you after all this time. I am so happy in the other world. I am with your grandfather and we spend all our time laughing and joking. We're having a ball.'

Jerzy went on to ask his grandmother half a dozen questions, and she answered each one until saying: 'Now, Jerzy, I must go. The angels are calling. I can answer only one more question.'

'Very well, Elka,' said Jerzy hesitantly.' Answer me this if you will: when did you learn to speak English?'

Ruddy Family

When an elderly man went to a new health centre for the first time, the doctor was immediately struck by the patient's extraordinarily ruddy complexion.

'It's high blood pressure, doctor,' explained the man. 'It comes from my family.'

'Your mother's side or your father's?' asked the doctor.

'Neither,' replied the man. 'It's from my wife's family.'

The doctor looked puzzled. 'I'm sorry, but I don't see how you can get high blood pressure from your wife's family.'

The man said: 'You should try spending a weekend with them!'

Last Respects

It was a hot summer afternoon and an old-timer and his wife were sitting serenely in their rocking chairs on the porch at the side of their house when they heard a funeral procession pass by the front door.

'That'll be old Jethro's funeral,' said the husband. 'They reckon it's the biggest there's been around here this century.'

'I'd like to have seen it,' said the wife.

'Me, too. After all, he was the best man at our wedding.'

'That's right. We've known him for years. It would have been good to have paid our last respects... Shame we ain't facing that way!'

Long Walks

Asked by a reporter how he had managed to live to the age of 100, an old man explained: 'Well, son, I got married when I was twenty-one. The wife and I decided that if ever we argued the loser should take a long walk to cool off. So I guess I've benefited from seventy-nine years of fresh air.'

Customer Satisfaction

Shopping at his local supermarket, an elderly gentleman went to the meat counter to buy a pack of boneless chicken breasts but was disappointed because they were all too small. So he complained to the butcher and she promised to pack up some more and to have them ready for him by the time he had finished his shopping.

He continued with the rest of his shopping until a few aisles further on, he heard her voice boom out over the public address system: 'Will the gentleman who was looking for bigger breasts please meet me at the back of the store.'

Mystery Benefactor

Returning home a day early from an out-of-town business trip, a man caught a taxi from the airport in the early hours of the morning. On the cab journey, he confided to the driver that he thought his wife was having an affair. As they pulled up outside his house, the businessman asked the driver: 'Would you come inside with me and be a witness?'

The driver agreed, and they both crept into the

bedroom. The man then turned on the lights, pulled back the blanket and, sure enough, his wife was naked in bed with another man.

In a fit of jealousy, the businessman pulled out a gun and threatened to shoot his wife's lover.

'Don't do it,' she begged. 'This man has been very generous. Who do you think paid for the new car I bought you for your birthday? Who do you think paid for our new boat? Who do you think paid for the deposit on this house? He did!'

His mind in turmoil, the husband looked over at the cab driver and asked: 'What would you do in a case like this?'

The cabbie said: 'I think I'd cover him up before he catches cold.'

Maiden Flight

An elderly woman on her first plane trip found herself a nice window seat in a no smoking area. But no sooner had she settled down than a man appeared and insisted that it was his seat.

Despite a lengthy argument, she flatly refused to move and told him to go away.

'Very well, madam,' he said. 'If that's the way you want it, you fly the plane!'

Never Judge a Book...

Having recently quit smoking, a middle-aged man was chewing on an unlit cigar when he visited a friend in hospital. As he stepped into the elevator, a woman told him firmly: 'There is no smoking in this hospital!'

'I'm not smoking, madam,' he replied.

'But you have a cigar in your mouth!'

'Yes, and I'm wearing Jockey shorts, but I'm not riding a horse!'

The Old Master

To prepare for starting a new office job, a young accountant spent a week with the retiring accountant whom he was replacing. He hoped to pick up a few tips from the old master and studied his daily routine intently.

Every morning the experienced accountant began the day by opening his desk drawer, taking out a frayed envelope and removing a yellowing piece of paper. He then read it, nodded his head sagely, returned the envelope to the drawer and started his day's work.

After the old man retired, the new boy could hardly wait to read for himself the message in the drawer. Surely the envelope must contain the secret to accounting success, a pearl of wisdom to be treasured for ever. The anticipation was so great that his hands were actually trembling as he opened the drawer and took out the mysterious envelope. And there, inside, on that aged piece of paper he read the following message:

'Debits in the column nearest the potted plant; credits in the column towards the door.'

Emergency Teeth

A senior speaker was about to address a public meeting when he realized that he had left his false teeth at home. So reluctantly he informed the lady who was chairing the meeting that he would be unable to give his speech as he had forgotten his teeth.

His plight was overheard by a man in the front row of the audience who immediately produced a pair of false teeth from his pocket and said: 'Here, try these.'

The speaker put the set of false teeth in his mouth but they were too tight.

'By pure chance, I have another pair,' said the man. 'Try these.'

The speaker put the second set in his mouth but

they were too loose. 'It's no good,' he sighed. 'I'll have to withdraw.'

'Wait,' said the man. 'It so happens that I have one more pair of false teeth in my pocket. See if these fit.'

So the speaker put them in his mouth and they fitted perfectly. 'Thank you so much,' he said. 'I've been looking for a good dentist.'

'I'm not a dentist,' said the man. 'I'm an undertaker.'

Plain English

A sixty-year-old man told the doctor that he was no longer able to help around the house like he used to. After the doctor had finished examining him, the man said: 'Now, doc, tell me in plain English what is wrong with me.'

'In plain English,' said the doctor, 'you're just lazy.'

'OK,' said the man, 'now give me the medical term so I can tell my wife.'

New Filling

Ted was in his seventies and had a job as a nightwatchman, and every evening before he set off for work his wife Muriel dutifully made him some sandwiches so that he could have something to eat around midnight. One morning when he returned home, she asked him: 'How were your sandwiches?'
'They were fine,' he replied.
'Are you sure they tasted OK?' she queried.
'Yes, they were very tasty.'
'You don't feel ill at all?' she added hesitantly.
'No, never felt better. Why?'
'Oh, no reason. Just asking…By the way, tomorrow you're going to have to clean your shoes with fish paste.'

Situation Vacant

An American tourist found himself in a sleepy country village and asked one of the locals the age of the oldest inhabitant.

'Well, sir,' replied the villager. 'We ain't got one now. He died last week.'

Eye Test

After putting off problems with her failing eyesight for several months, an elderly lady finally went to see an optician. He directed her to read various letters with the left eye while covering her right eye, then asked her to do the same with the right eye while covering her left eye. However she became so confused about the constant changes and which eye was which that eventually he took a paper lunch bag with a hole to see through, covered up the appropriate eye and asked her to read the letters.

As he did so, he noticed a look of disappointment on her face. 'Is something the matter?' he asked. 'There's no need to be sad about getting glasses at your time in life.'

'I know,' said the old lady, 'but it's just that I had my heart set on wire frames.'

Health Check

Two senior Jewish ladies, Sophie and Maureen, were shopping one afternoon when Sophie said: 'Wish me luck. My son finally met a girl and maybe they will get married. The only thing is my son said she has herpes. What is herpes?'

'I don't know,' said Maureen, 'but I have a medical dictionary at home so I'll look it up tonight.'

The next day the ladies met again.

'Did you find out about this herpes?' asked Sophie.

'Yes, it's OK' said Maureen. 'There's no need to worry. The book says it's a disease of the gentiles.'

Wrong Diagnosis

Two medical students were standing outside a store when they noticed an old man tottering along the street with his legs spread wide apart. The first student said to the second: 'I bet that old man has Goldman syndrome. That's how people with that condition walk.'

The second student begged to differ. 'No, I reckon he has Krakowsky syndrome. Remember, we learned about it in class? That's a classic case if ever I saw one!'

Since they were unable to agree, they decided to ask the old man. 'Excuse me,' they said. 'We're medical students and we couldn't help noticing the distinctive way you walk with your legs wide apart. But we can't agree on what syndrome you have. Could you tell us what it is, please?'

The old man said: 'I'll tell you, but first you must let me know what you think it is.'

The first student said: 'I think it's Goldman syndrome.'

The old man said: 'You thought, but you are wrong.'

The second student said: 'I think it's Krakowsky syndrome.'

The old man said: 'You thought, but you are wrong.'

'So what do you have?' they asked.

The old man said: 'I thought it was gas…but I was wrong.'

Taking Precautions

A couple in their eighties got married. On their honeymoon night while she slipped into her nightdress, he went into the bathroom. After he had been in there for fifteen minutes, she decided to check that he was OK. She found him struggling to put on a condom.

'Why are you putting on a condom?' she asked. 'I'm eighty-three – I can't possibly get pregnant!'

'Yes,' he said, 'but you know how dampness affects my arthritis.'

Wishful Thinking

'Now, Mrs Moore,' said the doctor, 'you say you have shooting pains in your neck, dizziness and constant nausea. Just for the record, how old are you?'

'I'm going to be thirty-nine on my next birthday,' she replied.

'Hmmmm,' said the doctor. 'You seem to be suffering from slight memory loss, too.'

Changing Times

1971: Long hair.
2011: Longing for hair.

1971: The perfect high.
2011: The perfect high-yield mutual fund.

1971: Moving to California because it's cool.
2011: Moving to California because it's warm.

1971: Getting out to a new, hip joint.
2011: Getting a new hip joint.

1971: Rolling Stones.
2011: Kidney stones.

1971: Growing pot.
2011: Growing pot belly.

1971: Take acid.
2011: Take antacid.

1971: Being a three-times-a-night man...in the bedroom.
2011: Being a three-times-a-night man...to the bathroom.

Words of Comfort

Shortly before the plane took off, an elderly lady passenger confided to the pilot: 'Excuse me, young man, but I've never flown before, and I'm very nervous. You will bring me down safely, won't you?'

'All I can say, ma'am,' replied the pilot, 'is that I've never left anyone up there yet!'

Any Questions

A woman decided to introduce her elderly mother to the magic of the Internet. 'We'll begin on the Ask Jeeves site, Mother. It's amazing. It will answer any question you have.'

'I don't believe you,' said the mother.

'It's true. Come on, give me a question to ask.'

The mother thought for a few moments and then said: 'How is Cousin Ada feeling today?'

Still Going Strong

A local newspaper interviewed an old man who had reached the age of 112. During the interview a pretty young woman served tea to the reporter, who noticed that the yard was full of children of all ages playing together.

'Are these your grandchildren?' asked the reporter.

'No,' said the old man, 'they're my children.'

'What about the young lady who brought my tea? Is she one of your children, too?'

'No,' said the old man, 'that's my wife.'

'Your wife?!' exclaimed the reporter. 'But she can't be more than twenty!'

'That's right,' said the old man.

The reporter was amazed. 'But you're 112! How can you have a sex life with a twenty-year-old?'

'We have sex every night,' explained the old man. 'Last thing at night, two of my boys help me on her and then first thing in the morning six of my boys help me off her.'

'Wait a minute,' said the reporter. 'Why does it only take two of your boys to put you on but it takes six of them to take you off?'

'Because,' said the old man belligerently, 'I fight them!'

Crazy Driver

A woman was visiting her father in a retirement home when another elderly man entered the ward, waving his arms about and making beeping noises.

'Excuse me,' said the woman. 'What are you doing?'

'I'm driving my car,' he replied breezily. 'Beep, beep!'

'But you're in the lounge of a retirement home,' she tried to explain. 'You're not in a car.'

'Don't tell him that,' cried the woman's father. 'He pays me ten dollars a week to clean it!'

A Mixed Message

William and Agnes met at a seniors' dance and had been going out for six weeks when it was Agnes's seventy-seventh birthday. To help him choose a suitable present, he asked Agnes's sister, Muriel, to come shopping with him.

In the department store William, acting on Muriel's advice, decided to buy Agnes an expensive pair of beige gloves while Muriel bought her a pair of white underpants. Unfortunately in the course of wrapping, the gifts became mixed up so that the parcel from William contained the underpants. Inside was a note which read:

'Dear Agnes, I chose these because I noticed you don't usually wear any when we go out. If it hadn't been for your sister, I would have chosen long ones with buttons, but she wears short ones that are easier to remove.

'I hope you like the shade. I know they're pale but the lady in the store showed me a pair she had been wearing for the past month and they were hardly soiled. I got her to try yours on for me and she looked really good in them.

'I wish I was there to put them on you for the first time, as no doubt other hands will come in contact with them before I see you again. Just think how many times I will kiss them over the coming months. I hope you wear them when we have dinner next Saturday. Yours affectionately, William.

'PS. The latest fashion is to wear them folded down with a little fur showing.'

Heavenly Guidance

An elderly priest approached a small boy in the street and said: 'Could you tell me where the post office is, please?'

The boy gave him directions, and the priest said: 'Thank you. If you come to my sermon tonight, I will tell you how to get to Heaven.'

'I don't think so,' said the boy. 'You don't even know how to get to the post office!'

No Need to Rush

As a transatlantic flight landed in New York, the pilot announced: 'Thank you for flying with us today. Enjoy your stay in New York and I hope we will have the pleasure of your company in the future.' Then, forgetting that his microphone was still switched on, he added: 'Now all I need is a nice cup of coffee and a woman.'

Hearing the gaffe, a pretty young flight attendant rushed up the gangway toward the cockpit. Halfway up the aisle an old lady patted her on the arm and said: 'Don't hurry, dear. Give him time to drink his coffee.'

Passing the Time

A neighbour who still worked for a living asked the retired man next door how he managed to pass the time and make his days interesting.

'We always find something to do,' said the retired man. 'Take the other day. My wife and I went into a shop in town. We were only in there five minutes but when we came out there was a cop writing out a parking ticket. We went up to him and said: "Come on, officer, how about giving a senior citizen a break?"'

'He ignored us and continued writing the ticket, so I called him a little Hitler. He glared at me and started writing another ticket for having worn tyres. This made my wife so angry that she called him an idiot. He finished writing the second ticket and put it on the windscreen with the first. Then he began writing a third ticket. This went on for about fifteen minutes. The more we abused him, the more tickets he wrote.'

'Didn't that bother you?' asked the neighbour.

'Not at all,' said the retired man. 'We'd travelled into town by bus!'

Table Manners

An elderly lady went to the doctor for a check-up. She said: 'Doctor, my husband and I haven't made love for years, so is there anything you can give him to increase his sex drive?'

'Have you tried giving him Viagra?' asked the doctor.

'He doesn't like taking tablets, even when he has a headache.'

'Well, crush it into a powder and stir it into his coffee. He won't notice it.'

Two weeks later, the woman returned. 'How did it go?' asked the doctor.

'It was terrible, doctor, terrible. I slipped the Viagra into his coffee like you said, and he just got up and ripped the clothes off me right there. We made mad love on the table – it was the best sex I've had in nearly twenty years.'

'So what's the problem?' asked the doctor.

The woman replied: 'I can't ever show my face in that restaurant again.'

Cold Case

A little old lady walked up to a police officer and said: 'Officer, I was molested by a stranger. It happened in the park and it went on for twenty minutes.'

'Can you tell me exactly when this incident took place?' asked the officer.

'Fifteen years ago,' replied the old lady.

'Why are you telling me this now?'

She smiled: 'I just like to talk about it once in a while.'

Age Gap

An eighty-year-old man married a twenty-year-old girl and, to the amazement of both families, a year later she gave birth.

A nurse at the hospital congratulated the proud father, saying: 'This is incredible. How do you do it at your age?'

'Well,' he answered, 'you've got to keep the old motor running.'

The following year, the young bride had another baby. The same nurse said to the old man: 'You're amazing. How do you do it?'

Again he replied: 'You've got to keep the old motor running.'

His wife gave birth for a third time the following year, prompting the nurse to tell him: 'You really are an amazing character!'

'You've got to keep the old motor running,' he replied.

'Well, perhaps you'd better change the oil,' said the nurse. 'This one's black.'

The Nervous Patient

Anxiously pacing the hospital corridor, a man was becoming increasingly nervous about his imminent operation.

'What's the matter?' asked his wife. 'You've been calm all week. Why are you suddenly getting so worked up?'

He replied: 'One of the nurses said, "It's a very simple operation; don't get yourself in such a state. I'm sure it will be all right."'

'She was merely trying to reassure you,' said his wife. 'What's so frightening about that?'

The husband said: 'She was talking to the surgeon!'

Friendly Advice

Henry complained to his friend Arnold that sex with his wife was becoming routine and boring.

'Be creative, Henry,' advised Arnold. 'Break up the monotony. Why don't you try playing "doctor" for an hour? That's what I do.'

'Sounds great,' said Henry. 'But how do you make it last for an hour?'

Arnold replied: 'Just keep her in the waiting room for forty-five minutes.'

The Afterlife

An elderly widow was worried whether her late husband had made it to Heaven, so she decided to try and contact his spirit by holding a séance. Sure enough, after a few minutes her husband's voice was heard to answer:
'Hello, Margaret. It's me, Edgar.'
'Edgar,' she said joyously. 'I just need to know if you're happy in the afterlife. What's it like there?'
'It's more beautiful than I ever imagined,' replied Edgar. 'The sky is bluer, the air is cleaner and the fields are much greener than I expected. And the only things we do all day long are eat and sleep, sleep and eat, over and over.'
'I'm so glad you made it to Heaven,' she said.
'Heaven?' said Edgar. 'I'm not in Heaven. I'm a buffalo in Montana!'

No Easy Touch

A counterfeiter decided to pass off his phony eighteen-dollar bills in a remote country town. So he drove for hours until he found a little store that suited his purposes.

He went up to the counter and handed one of the bogus bills to the old man at the cash desk.

'Could you change this for me, please?' he asked.

The elderly clerk looked at the bill for a few seconds and then smiled: 'Of course I can. Would you prefer two nine-dollar bills or three six-dollar bills?'

The Lost Toupee

A middle-aged man decided to conceal his baldness by buying a hairpiece, which he hoped would make him more attractive to women. That night he took it for its first outing to a singles bar, where he picked up a pretty young woman and took her back to his apartment.

To get her in the mood, he switched off the lights but as they started fumbling passionately in the dark, he realized to his horror that his toupee had fallen off. He began groping frantically for it, hoping to put it back on his head before the girl saw that he was really bald.

In his desperation to find the wig, he inadvertently ran his hands up the girl's legs.

'Oh! That's it!' she gasped in ecstasy.

'No, it isn't,' he said, momentarily forgetting himself. 'Mine's got a side parting.'

Tired of Waiting

Two women were complaining about hospital waiting lists. One said: 'My ninety-year-old mother has been waiting over a year for her operation.'

'That's terrible,' said the other woman. 'What an awful way to treat someone of that age.'

'I know,' said the first woman. 'It got so bad that at one point I even said to her, "Mum, are you sure you really need bigger boobs?"'

Age Concern

A female gambler was having a bad day at the casino. Down to her last fifty dollars, she exclaimed in exasperation: 'What rotten luck I've had this evening! How can I get out of the mess I'm in?'

A man standing next to her at the roulette table suggested: 'Why don't you play your age? You never know, it might bring you luck.' The man then wandered off. But moments later he heard a tremendous commotion at the roulette table. Hurrying back, he found the woman lying unconscious on the floor with the table operator kneeling over her.

'What happened?' he asked. 'Is she all right?'

The operator replied: 'I don't know. She put all her money on thirty-nine, and forty-seven came up. Then she just fainted...'

Feisty Couple

An elderly couple were sitting quietly on the porch in their rocking chairs when the old man suddenly reached across and slapped his wife in the face.

'What was that for?' she demanded.

'That's for forty years of lousy sex!'

She didn't say anything, but a few minutes later she slapped him back.

'What was that for?' he cried.

'That's for knowing the difference!'

The Cold Caller

An old lady hated salespeople who went cold-calling door-to-door, so when one knocked at her house she told him bluntly that she was not interested in his product and slammed the door in his face. But to her horror, the door didn't close and instead bounced back open. So she tried for a second time, with more force, but the door still wouldn't close and bounced back open again.

Convinced that the salesman was deliberately putting his foot in the door to prevent her shutting it, she reared back to give the door an almighty slam that would finally teach him a lesson.

But as she went to do so, the salesman interrupted: 'Madam, before you do that again, you might want to move your cat.'

Fading Memory

Two old men were talking about their distant youths. One said: 'Can you remember the name of the first woman you ever kissed?' His friend answered: 'I can't even remember the name of the last one!'

Say it with Flowers

A married man in his fifties walked into a florist's and said: 'I'd like to buy some flowers.'

'Certainly, sir,' said the florist. 'What sort of flowers would you like?'

'I'm not really sure,' said the man.

'Well, perhaps I can help,' suggested the florist. 'What exactly have you done?'

Past Conquests

Bert and Sid were sitting on a park bench. A blonde woman walked by, and Bert said to Sid: 'Ever sleep with a blonde?'

'Many a time,' said Sid. 'Many a time.'

A brunette then walked by. Bert asked Sid: 'Ever sleep with a brunette?'

'Many a time,' replied Sid. 'Many a time.'

Then a redhead walked by, and Bert asked Sid: 'Ever sleep with a redhead?'

Sid answered: 'Not a wink.'

The Slippery Slope

A young boy was looking through the family photo album and asked his mother: 'Who's this guy on the beach with you with all the muscles and curly hair?'

'That's your father,' she said.

'OK,' said the boy. 'Then who's that bald-headed fat old man who lives with us now?'

Smoking Aid

An old woman found a condom in her grandson's apartment and asked what it was.
'It's a condom,' replied her grandson sheepishly.
'What do you use it for?' asked the old woman.
The grandson was too embarrassed to admit the truth, so he said: 'I use it to keep my cigarettes dry when I smoke in the rain.'
'That's a great idea,' said the old woman. And she went straight to the chemist and asked for a condom.
'What size would you like?' asked the pharmacist.
The old woman replied: 'Big enough to fit a Camel.'

Weight Worries

Concerned that she had started to put on weight since turning fifty, a woman sought help from a therapist. She told him that no matter how hard she tried, she had never been able to stick to diets and always gave up after a few months. He told her: 'The key to a happy and successful life is: always finish what you start.'

She took his advice on board and when she returned for her next appointment, she had a much more optimistic outlook.

'I feel better already,' she told the therapist. 'So far today I've finished a box of chocolates, a packet of biscuits and a vanilla sponge cake.'

Rise and Shine

One Monday morning, a mother went in to wake her son and tell him that it was time to go to school.

'I'm not going,' he said in a sulky manner.

'Why not?' she asked.

'Two reasons: They don't like me and I don't like them.'

His mother said: 'Well, I'll give you two reasons why you should go to school: Firstly, you're fifty-nine years old; and secondly, you're the school principal!'

Family Gathering

An elderly tailor was on his death bed with his three sons around him.

'Michael, are you here?' asked the old man.

'Yes, Father, I am by your side,' said Michael.

'And you, Benjamin?'

'Yes, Father,' said Benjamin. 'Rest assured, I am here with you.'

'And, Morris, have you come as well?'

'Yes, Father,' replied Morris. 'I am here, too.'

Hearing this, the old man threw up his hands in horror and cried: 'So who is minding the shop?'

Raisin Bread

The proprietor of a general store hired a young female clerk who wore very short skirts to work. One day a young man came into the store and asked for some raisin bread. Since the raisin bread was located on the top shelf, the clerk had to climb a stepladder to reach it, which gave the young man the chance to look up her skirt. He enjoyed the view so much that when she came down, he suddenly remembered he needed more raisin bread – merely as an excuse to get her to climb the ladder again.

By now the other male customers in the store had realized what was going on and they, too, took it in turns to ask for raisin bread. Each time the girl climbed the ladder to fetch the raisin bread they got to see up her skirt. After her seventh climb, she was beginning to feel exhausted. From the top step, she looked down at the group of men and spotted an old man, who had yet to be served, gazing up at her. In a bid to save herself another trip, she asked him: 'Is yours raisin, too?'

'No,' replied the old man, 'but it's starting to twitch!'

Birthday Prayer

A boy was heard praying in a loud voice a week before his eighth birthday: 'Dear God, I pray that I will get a computer game for my birthday.'

'Why are you shouting?' asked his mother. 'God isn't deaf.'

'I know,' said the boy, 'but Grandma is.'

Dress Code

Two elderly ladies were discussing an upcoming dance at their local country club. One said: 'We're supposed to wear something that matches our husband's hair, so I'm wearing a black dress, black underwear and black shoes to match my husband's black hair.'

'Oh, my!' said the other woman, blushing. 'I'd better not go.'

Encounter with a Lion

A ninety-year-old man was being interviewed on radio about his life as an explorer.

'I'll never forget my first trip to Africa,' he began. 'It was back in 1946, and I was travelling south of Nairobi. There were five of us in the party, but somehow I had become separated from the others. Trying to find my way back to the jeep, I headed down this overgrown track. I had only gone a hundred yards when I heard a rustling sound in the bushes. Then suddenly the biggest lion I had ever seen jumped out of the bushes at me like this: "ROOAAARRR!" I tell you, I just messed my pants.'

'I'm not surprised,' said the interviewer. 'I would have messed my pants, too, if a lion jumped out at me.'

'No, not then,' said the old man. 'Just now when I went "ROOAAARRR!"'

Carry on Talking

On a visit to the cinema, a man was struggling to hear the dialogue above the incessant chatter of the two elderly women sitting directly in front of him. Unable to bear it any longer, he tapped one of the women on the shoulder.

'Excuse me,' he said. 'I can't hear.'

'I should hope not,' she replied sharply. 'This is a private conversation.'

Passion Killer

A middle-aged married couple were members of a tour party that went scuba-diving off the coast of Florida. After spending an hour in the water, everyone got back on the boat except for the wife and a handsome young man. As she continued to explore underwater, she noticed that wherever she swam, he did, too. She continued diving for another twenty minutes, and so did he, virtually shadowing her every move.

She felt extremely flattered by his attention, and as she took off her scuba-diving gear, she coyly asked him why he had remained in the water for so long.

'I couldn't get out until you did,' he replied curtly. 'I'm the lifeguard.'

Revenge Is Sweet

An old man had an appointment to see a urologist who shared an office with several other doctors. The waiting room was filled with patients. The old man approached the reception desk. The receptionist was a large imposing woman who looked like a wrestler. He gave her his name, and she replied in a loud voice: 'Oh yes, you want to see the doctor about impotence, right?'

As the heads of all the patients turned around to look at him, the old man felt acutely embarrassed. But thinking on his feet, he told the receptionist in an equally loud voice: 'No, I've come to enquire about a sex change operation – and I'd like the same doctor who did yours!'

Photo Session

Twin sisters had just turned 100 years old, so the nursing home where they lived notified the local newspaper editor who sent a photographer to take pictures of the two old ladies. One of the twins was hard of hearing but the other could hear quite well.

The photographer asked them to sit on the sofa. The deaf one said to her twin: 'What did he say?'

'We gotta sit over there on the sofa,' said the other.

'Now move a little closer together,' said the photographer.

'What did he say?' asked the deaf one.

'He said we have to squeeze together a little.'

So they wiggled up close together.

'Just hold that for a second,' said the photographer. 'I've just got to focus.'

'What did he say?' bellowed the deaf one.

'He says he's gonna focus.'

'Oh my God!' exclaimed the deaf twin. 'Both of us?!'

A Cure for Snoring

Irritated by her husband's persistent snoring, a woman called on the family doctor to ask him if there was anything he could do to relieve her suffering.

'Well,' said the doctor, 'there is one operation I can perform that will cure your husband, but it really is rather expensive. It will cost $5,000 down payment, followed by payments of $1,500 every month for twenty-four months.'

'What is it?' asked the wife, mystified.

'A new sports car,' replied the doctor.

'A new sports car? How on earth will that help cure my

husband's snoring?'

'Simple,' said the doctor. 'He won't be able to sleep at night for worrying about how he's going to pay for it!'

Grandma Knows Best

A man joined a nudist colony. After a few weeks he received a letter from his mother asking him to send her a current photograph. Too embarrassed to tell her that he lived in a nudist colony, he cut a picture in half and sent her the top half.

A month later he received another letter, this time asking him to send a photo to his grandmother. So he cut another photo in half, but accidentally sent the bottom half to the old lady. He was horrified to realize that he had sent the wrong part, but then remembered that his grandmother's eyesight was so bad that she probably wouldn't notice.

The following week he received a letter back from his grandmother. It said: 'Thank you for the photo. But I think you should change your hairstyle – it makes your nose look long.'

Weather Forecast

An elderly lady phoned her local TV station to complain about the weather forecaster. 'What's the problem?' asked the TV station press officer.

The old lady said: 'Your weather forecaster said there would be six inches of snow last night, but when I woke up this morning there was miles of it!'

Signs That You May Be Carrying a Few Extra Pounds in Middle Age

- You've forgotten what it was like to be able to cross your legs.

- When you go up the stairs, the house shakes.

- You realize the rolls on your arms aren't muscles.

- Even your shadow has stretch marks.

- One of your legs is as big as a person.

- You can pinch a lot more than an inch.

- You can no longer sit on chairs that have arms.

- You bump into things that you never did before.

- The car seat belt won't expand any further.

- When you get in a pool, the water comes out.

- Your favourite clothing store has the name 'tents' in the title.

- Chairs make rude noises when you sit in them.

- You notice that they just don't make towels as big as they used to.

- You can't step in an elevator with other people because of the weight limit.

- You don't fit on the toilet seat.

- The back of your neck looks like a pack of hot dogs.

Cold Comfort

A couple had been married for thirty-three years but eventually the husband's strange behaviour forced the woman to turn to a psychiatrist for help.

'Doctor,' she said, 'I'm really worried about my husband. He thinks he's a refrigerator.'

'It could be worse,' said the psychiatrist. 'After all a refrigerator is a fairly harmless contraption.'

'That may be true,' she said. 'But he sleeps with his mouth open and the light keeps me awake.'

A Sore Point

After lying on the beach on a hot summer's day, a senior man suffered severe sunburn. His skin was red, sore and starting to blister, so he was taken to hospital. Anything that touched his body left him in agony. After examining him, the doctor prescribed a mild sedative and Viagra.

'What good will Viagra do him in his condition?' asked the nurse.

The doctor replied: 'It will keep the sheet off him.'

Finders Keepers

An elderly couple who were childhood sweethearts had married and settled down in their old neighbourhood. To celebrate their fiftieth wedding anniversary, they walked to their old school. There, they held hands as they found the desk on which he had written 'Harry Loves Susan' all those years ago.

On their way back home, a bag full of cash fell from a passing armoured car and landed at their feet. The wife picked up the bag and, unsure what to do with it, took it home where it was found to contain £60,000.

'We have to give it back,' said the husband.

'No way!' she said. 'Finders keepers!' So she put the money back in the bag and hid it in the attic.

The next day two policemen called at the house while making door-to-door inquiries about the missing cash. One knocked at the door and asked: 'Pardon me, but did either of you find any money that fell out of an armoured car yesterday?'

'No,' said the wife.

'She's lying,' said her husband. 'She's hidden it in the attic.'

'Don't listen to him,' she snapped. 'He's getting senile.'

The agents were unsure who to believe but decided to sit down and question the husband. One said: 'Right, sir, tell us the story right from the beginning.'

The husband said: 'Well, when Susan and I were walking home from school yesterday...'

The policeman looked at his partner and said: 'Let's go. We're wasting time here!'

The Wrong Card

On opening his new store, a man received a bouquet of flowers but was dismayed to see that the attached message read: 'With Deepest Sympathy'. So he phoned the florist to ask about the card.

'Oh, dear,' said the elderly florist.'I must have accidentally sent you the wrong card.'

'Don't worry,' said the man. 'These things happen.'

'No, you don't understand,' said the florist. 'I've sent your card to a funeral party.'

'What did it say?'

'Congratulations on your new location.'

Ladies Who Lunch

For over forty years, Betty and Rose had met up once a week for lunch. Eventually Betty said: 'All we ever seem to talk about over lunch are the trivial things in life – like buying new cushions, what the weather forecast is or what colour you should paint your lounge. Next time we meet why don't we have a serious discussion about world affairs?'

'That's a good idea,' said Rose.

So the following week while they were waiting for lunch to arrive, Rose said: 'Go on, Betty, you start the serious political debate.'

'OK,' said Betty. 'What do you think about the situation with Red China?'

Rose replied: 'Not much – it won't go with your green tablecloth.'

Sharp Practice

A little old lady was walking along the street, dragging two plastic garbage bags, one in each hand. There was a hole in one of the bags, leaving a trail of twenty-pound notes in her wake. Seeing this, a police officer stopped her and said: 'Ma'am, there are twenty-pound notes falling out of that bag.'

'Oh, thank you,' said the little old lady. 'I'll go back and collect them.'

'Hang on just a minute,' said the officer. 'Would you mind telling me how you came by all that money?'

'It's not stolen, if that's what you're thinking,' said the little old lady. 'You see, my garden backs on to the car park of the football stadium and whenever there's a game a lot of fans come and pee in the bushes, right on to my nice flower beds. So I deliberately stand behind the bushes with a big pair of shears and every time someone sticks his wotnot through, I say: "Twenty pounds or off it comes!"'

'Hey, that's the best idea I've heard in ages!' laughed the officer. 'You teach them a lesson! By the way, what's in the other bag?'

'Well,' said the little old lady, 'not all of them pay up.'

Soothing Words

A man was run over by a truck on a busy city street. As he lay dying, a crowd gathered around him to see if they could help.

'A priest! A priest! Will somebody fetch me a priest!'

gasped the dying man. A policeman checked among the onlookers, but there was no religious man of any kind present.

'A priest, please!' the dying man repeated.

Then out of the crowd stepped a little old man. 'Officer,' he said to the policeman, 'I'm not a priest, I'm not even a Catholic, but for the past thirty-six years I have lived behind St Mary's Catholic Church, and every night I overhear the Catholic litany. Perhaps I can be of some comfort to this poor man.'

The policeman thought it was a good idea and took the old man over to where the accident victim lay dying. The pensioner knelt down gingerly, leaned over the man and announced in a solemn voice: 'One little duck, number two; doctor's orders, number nine; two fat ladies, eighty-eight...'

A Shopping Experience

A senior woman was telling her neighbour about the new supermarket that had opened on the edge of town.

'It's all very state-of-the-art and designed to make shopping a natural and relaxing experience. It has an automatic water mister to keep all the fruit fresh. Just before it switches on, you hear the sound of distant thunder and smell the aroma of fresh rain. As you approach the milk aisle, you hear cows mooing and there's the scent of fresh hay. As you get near the eggs, you hear hens clucking and the air is filled with the delicious smell of bacon and eggs frying. And the vegetable department features the aroma of fresh buttered corn.'

'It sounds wonderful,' enthused the neighbour.

'Yes, it is, but I don't buy toilet paper there any more.'

Comparing Perfumes

An old woman was riding in an elevator in a posh New York apartment building when a beautiful young woman stepped in smelling of expensive perfume. She turned to the old woman and said arrogantly: 'Romance by Ralph Lauren, $150 an ounce.'

At the next floor, another beautiful young woman got in, also smelling of expensive perfume. She turned to the old woman and declared haughtily: 'Chanel No. 5, $200 an ounce.'

The old woman felt so intimidated that as she got out of

the elevator at the next floor she accidentally broke wind. Turning to the two young women, she said: 'Broccoli, forty-nine cents a pound.'

Bowl of Rice

Taking flowers to a cemetery, a woman noticed an old Chinese man placing a bowl of rice on a nearby grave.

Thinking it a strange form of memorial, she said: 'When exactly do you expect your friend to come up and eat the rice?'

The Chinese man replied: 'The same time your friend comes up to smell the flowers!'

Horns of a Dilemma

A group of seniors from the city decided to go on a day trip to a working farm in the country. Since most of them had lived in the city all their lives and had never been near a farm, they thought it would be a new experience.

Dressed for the part, they arrived in their minibus and were greeted by the farmer. As they looked around the various barns and outhouses, one woman was intrigued by an animal she spotted.

'Excuse me,' she called to the farmer, 'can you explain to us why this cow doesn't have any horns?'

The farmer cocked his head for a moment, and then explained patiently: 'Well, madam, cattle can do a lot of damage with horns. So sometimes we keep them trimmed down with a hacksaw. Or when they're young, we can put a few drops of acid where their horns would normally grow, and that stops the horns developing. And of course there are some breeds of cattle that never even grow horns. But the reason this particular cow doesn't have any horns, madam, is because it's a horse.'

Lopsided

An old man went to the doctor: 'I don't know what's wrong with me, doctor,' he said. 'My right ear is always warmer than my left one.'
'Yes, I can see what the problem is,' said the doctor, examining him. 'You need to adjust your toupee.'

Medicinal Drink

Two elderly men walked into a bar. 'Why don't we have a Guinness?' suggested one. 'It's supposed to put lead in your pencil.'

'I guess we could try,' said the other. 'Although, to be honest, I've got nobody to write to.'

What's His Secret?

A man walked into a police station and demanded to speak with the burglar who had broken into his house the previous night.

'You'll get your chance in court,' said the desk sergeant.

'No, you don't understand,' said the man. 'I want to know how he got into the house in the middle of the night without waking my wife. I've been trying to do that for the past twenty years!'

Sea Cruise

To celebrate a couple's fiftieth wedding anniversary, the wife suggested that they go on a cruise together. 'We could go somewhere for a week and make passionate love like we did when we were young.'

The husband thought it was a good idea, so he went to the pharmacy and bought a bottle of seasickness pills and a tube of lubricant. When he returned home, his wife said: 'I've been thinking, there's no reason why we can't go away for a month.'

The husband agreed and went back to the pharmacist to buy four bottles of seasickness pills and another tube of lubricant. When he got back home, his wife said: 'Actually now that the kids have left home there's nothing to stop us cruising the world for six months.'

The husband agreed and returned to the pharmacist to buy twenty-four bottles of seasickness pills and six more tubes of lubricant.

The pharmacist said: 'Excuse me, sir, I don't mean to pry, but if it makes you that sick, why do you keep doing it?'

Botched Operation

When an elderly female patient regained consciousness after a difficult operation, the surgeon told her: 'I'm really sorry, but I'm afraid we're going to have to open you up again. You see, unfortunately I left my scalpel inside you.'

The woman looked at him and said: 'Well, if it's all the same to you, I'd prefer you to leave me alone and I'll buy you a new one.'

Shotgun Marriage

A little old lady walked into a Texas gun store and said: 'I'd like a rifle. It's for my husband.'

'Certainly,' said the sales clerk. 'Did he say what make he wanted?'

'No, he didn't,' said the little old lady.

'Did he say what calibre he wanted?'

'No, he didn't,' said the little old lady.

'Well, did he say what type of scope he wanted?'

'No, he didn't,' said the little old lady. 'In fact, he doesn't even know I'm going to shoot him yet!'

Keep Fit

An elderly lady was telling her friend that she had recently joined an aerobics class for seniors at the local fitness centre.

'How did it go?' asked the friend.

'Well, I bent, I twisted, I turned, I jumped up and down, and I perspired for half an hour, but by the time I'd finally got my leotard on, the class had ended.'

Wedding Night

When a ninety-four-year-old man married a twenty-one-year-old girl, the wedding guests privately feared that the wedding night might prove fatal because he was a frail old man and she was a vivacious young woman. But the next morning everyone was surprised to see the bride come down the main stairwell of the hotel very gingerly, step by step, and painfully bow-legged. Eventually she managed to hobble to the front desk.

Seeing the state of her, the clerk asked the bride: 'What on earth happened to you? You look as if you've gone ten rounds with Evander Holyfield?'

'It's my husband!' she gasped. 'Oh, my God! What a night! When he told me that he'd been saving up for seventy-five years, I thought he meant his money!'

Another Martini

A middle-aged man went into a bar and ordered a series of Martinis. After each one, he removed the olive and put it in a jar.

Eventually the bartender asked him: 'Why do you keep doing that?'

'Because,' replied the man in a slurred voice, 'my wife sent me out for a jar of olives.'

Flower Show Streaker

Joyce and Ethel were attending a flower show. After a few hours of looking around the various stalls, Joyce turned to Ethel and said: 'I'm bored. This place needs livening up a bit. I know what I'm going to do: I'm going to streak through the main marquee.'

'Joyce, you can't,' protested Ethel. 'Not at your age.'

'Just watch me!' said Joyce.

Unable to bear the sight of her friend embarrassing herself, Ethel waited outside while Joyce ran naked through the marquee accompanied by a tremendous roar from onlookers.

'What happened?' asked Ethel when Joyce reappeared.

'It was wonderful,' said Joyce. 'Everybody cheered and I won first prize for Best Dried Arrangement!'

Daredevil Grandma

Ben complained to his school friend that he hadn't slept a wink for the past two nights.

'Why's that?' asked his friend.

Ben explained: 'Grandma broke her leg. The doctor put it in plaster and told her not to walk up stairs. You should hear the noise she makes when she climbs the drainpipe!'

Lottery Win

An old man and his son eked out a meagre living on a mule farm. Then one day the son won £100,000 on the lottery. He told his father the good news, then rushed into town to collect his money. On his return he handed his father a fifty-pound note.

The father looked at the money for a moment and then said: 'Son, you know I've always been careful with what little money we had. I didn't spend it on whisky or women. In fact, I couldn't even afford a licence to marry your mother legally.'

The son was shocked by the revelation and yelled: 'Do you know what that makes me?!'

'Sure do,' said the father, fingering the fifty-dollar bill, 'and a damn cheap one at that!'

Three Hymns

One Sunday, a pastor asked his congregation to put a little extra in the collection plate and by way of incentive he said that whoever gave the most money would be able to select three hymns.

When the plates were returned, the pastor noticed that someone had contributed a $100 bill. So he asked the generous donor to put his or her hand up.

An elderly widow raised her hand. The pastor thanked her profusely, then asked her to come to the front and pick out three hymns. After slowly making her way to the front, her eyes lit up and pointing to three handsome young men in the congregation, she said gleefully: 'I'll have him, him and him.'

Something Fishy

An old lady who was hard of hearing went to the doctor to find out whether there was any risk of her getting pregnant again.

The doctor told her: 'Mrs Walker, you're seventy-three, and although one can never rule out an act of God, if you were to have a baby it would be a miracle.'

When she arrived home, her husband asked her what the doctor had said.

'I didn't quite catch it all,' she admitted, 'but it sounded a bit fishy; something about an act of cod, and if I had a baby it would be a mackerel.'

Moving Tribute

Three old men were discussing death. The first said: 'When you're lying in the casket and your friends and family are mourning you, what would you most like to hear them say about you? I know what I'd like to hear. I'd like to hear them say, "He was a great doctor and a wonderful husband and father."'

The second man said: 'I'd like to hear them say, "He was an inspirational teacher who made a difference to so many lives.'''

The third man said: 'I'd like to hear them say, "Look, he's moving!"'

The Smile Test

A self-important sex therapist boasted that he could tell how often people had sex simply by looking at the smile on their face. To test his theory, he filled a room with people of different ages and went down the line, asking each one to smile. His deductions proved correct in every case until he arrived at the last person in line, a sixty-five-year-old man, who was grinning from ear to ear.

'Twice a day?' guessed the therapist.

'No,' said the man.

'Once a day?'

'No.'

'Once a week?'

'No.'

'Once a month?'

'No.'

'Once every six months?'

'No.'

'Once a year?'

'Yes.'

'Well, what the hell have you got to look so happy about?' snapped the therapist, angry that his theory wasn't working.

The man beamed: 'Tonight's the night!'

Miracle Cure

Bent double with arthritis, an old lady shuffled into the doctor's office, leaning on her cane. Half an hour later, she emerged walking erect with her head held high.

Another patient in the waiting room exclaimed: 'It's a miracle. You walked in bent in half and now you're walking straight. What did the doctor do to cure your arthritis?'

The old lady said: 'He gave me a longer walking stick.'

Mystery Solved

A retired gentleman started calling into his local pharmacy every week to purchase a box of fifteen condoms. After six months of this routine, the shop assistant's curiosity got the better of him.

'Excuse me, sir,' he said, 'but you get through a lot of condoms for someone your age. You must have the stamina of a bull.'

'Oh, they're not for sex,' said the old man. 'I haven't had sex in ten years.'

'So what do you do with all those condoms?' asked the clerk.

'If you must know, I feed them to my Jack Russell terrier so that he poos in little plastic bags.'

Good Deed

Four Boy Scouts told their scoutmaster that they had performed their good deed for the day.

'What did you do?' asked the scoutmaster.

'We helped an old lady across the street,' they said.

'That's very commendable,' said the scoutmaster, 'but did it take all four of you to do that?'

'Yes,' they replied. 'She didn't want to go.'

Headache Remedy

John suffered from repeated headaches and eventually decided to go and seek medical advice. The doctor told him: 'The good news is that I can cure your headache; the bad news is that it will require castration. You see, you have an extremely rare condition which causes your testicles to press on your spine, and the pressure creates an excruciating headache. The only way to relieve the pressure is to remove the testicles.'

John was shocked and depressed by the diagnosis but rather than dwell on his misfortune, he decided to undergo the necessary surgery as soon as possible.

So he had the operation, and after leaving hospital

realized that it was the first time in over fifteen years that he didn't have a headache. Although only too aware of what he had lost, he resolved to make a fresh start and when he saw a clothes shop, he decided to go in.

Once inside, he told the elderly tailor: 'I'd like to buy a new suit.'

The tailor eyed him up and down briefly and said: 'Let's see…size forty-four long.'

John laughed. 'That's right. How did you know?'

'Been in the business sixty years,' smiled the tailor.

John tried on the suit. It fitted perfectly.

As John admired himself in the mirror, the tailor asked: 'How about a new shirt?'

'Sure,' said John. 'Why not?'

The tailor eyed him before announcing: 'Thirty-four-inch sleeve and sixteen neck.'

'Amazing!' said John. 'You're right again. How did you know?'

'Been in the business sixty years,' smiled the tailor.

John tried on the shirt and it was a perfect fit. As he adjusted the collar in the mirror, the tailor thought he would push his luck and asked: 'How about new shoes?'

'Sure,' said John.

The tailor glanced at John's feet. 'Hmmm, 10½ E, I think.'

'That's right,' said John. 'How did you know?'

'Been in the business sixty years,' smiled the tailor.

John put on the shoes and they fitted perfectly. As John tried them out by walking around the shop, the tailor, keen to make another sale, asked: 'How about some new underwear?'

John thought for a second and said: 'Sure.'

The tailor stepped back, eyed John's waist and said: 'Let's see…size thirty-six.'

John laughed: 'Ha! I got you! I've worn size thirty-two since I was eighteen years old.'

The tailor shook his head. 'You can't wear a size thirty-two. Not with your build. Size thirty-two underpants would press your testicles up against the base of your spine and give you one hell of a headache.'

Hidden Meaning

As the guest of honour at a distinguished dinner party, the speaker was about to begin his speech when his wife, who was sitting at the other end of the table, sent him a piece of paper with the word 'KISS' scribbled on it.

A guest seated next to the speaker said: 'Your wife has sent you a KISS before you begin your speech. She must love you very much. You're a wonderful advertisement for thirty years of marriage.'

'You don't know my wife!' answered the speaker. 'The letters stand for "Keep It Short, Stupid."'

Not an Enemy in the World

During a church service, the minister asked his congregation: 'How many of you have forgiven your enemies?' Everyone held up their hands except for one little old lady.

'Miss Perry,' said the minister, 'are you not willing to forgive your enemies?'

'I don't have any,' she replied, smiling sweetly.

'Miss Perry, that is most unusual,' said the minister. 'How old are you, if you don't mind me asking?'

'Ninety-six,' she replied.

'That's incredible!' smiled the minister. 'Miss Perry, would you be so kind as to come down here and tell the rest of our congregation how a person can live ninety-six years and not have an enemy in the world?'

The sweet little old lady tottered down the aisle, faced the congregation and declared: 'It's simple. I outlived the bitches.'

The Perfect Gift

A little old lady had extremely poor eyesight. Her three sons were devoted to her and each wanted to prove that he was the kindest. So the first son, who was very wealthy, bought her a mansion. The second son, who was fairly wealthy, bought her a Rolls-Royce with a chauffeur. The third, who was much poorer than the other two, bought her a designer parrot, which as the result of ten years' intensive training, could recite the entire Bible. Knowing that his mother was a keen churchgoer, he thought the bird would be an imaginative gift for her.

The old lady told the first son: 'The house is lovely but it's too big for me, and with my terrible eyesight, I'm afraid I'd lose my way around.'

She told the second son: 'The car is beautiful, but my eyesight is so bad that I can't drive and even as a passenger I wouldn't be able to enjoy the view.'

Turning to the third son, she said warmly: 'I just want to thank you for the most thoughtful gift. That chicken was delicious.'

Teething Troubles

A couple in their eighties got married. On their wedding night, the groom spent ages in the bathroom.

'What are you doing in there?' asked his new wife. 'What's taking you so long?'

'I'm brushing my teeth,' he replied.

She called out: 'It doesn't take that long to brush your teeth.'

He yelled back: 'But I'm brushing yours, too.'

Old House

A medium was performing on stage in front of a captivated audience. The theatre descended into darkness, the medium entered a trance-like state and after a couple of minutes of eerie silence, he called out plaintively: 'Does the name Lakeview Cottage mean anything to anyone here?'

'Well I never!' cried a woman on the front row. 'That was the name of my mother's old house!'

The medium said: 'Well, my dear, I think I can contact her.'

The woman said: 'So can I. She's sitting next to me!'

Any Questions?

An elderly woman visited a gynaecologist for the first time. He was young and efficient and gave her a thorough examination which left her feeling rather embarrassed. When he had finished he told her to get dressed. He then gave her the results of his examination in great detail before asking her whether she had any questions.

'Just one,' said the old woman.

'What's that?' he asked.

'Does your mother know what you do for a living?'

Embarrassing Journey

A businessman was travelling on a train when he suddenly broke wind very loudly. In an attempt to cover his acute embarrassment, he tried to make conversation with the elderly lady sitting opposite him and asked her: 'Do you happen to have today's paper?'

'No,' she replied softly, 'but at the next station I'll try and grab you a handful of leaves.'

Decision Making

A local newspaper reporter was interviewing a couple who had been married for sixty years. 'What's the secret to such a long and happy marriage?' he asked.

'Well,' replied the husband, 'it's like this. The man makes all the big decisions and the woman just makes the little decisions.'

'Does that really work?' said the reporter.

'Oh, yes,' said the husband. 'Sixty years and so far not one big decision!'

Anniversary Treat

A couple had just been out for dinner to celebrate their twenty-fifth wedding anniversary. On their way home, the wife thanked her husband for a wonderful evening.

'Oh, it's not over yet,' he said, and once inside the house he presented her with a little black velvet box.

She opened it with eager anticipation, only to find two small pills. 'What are these?' she asked, puzzled.

'They're aspirin,' he replied.

'But I haven't got a headache.'

'Gotcha!'

Friends Reunited

A group of fifteen-year-old schoolgirls decided to meet up for dinner. They discussed where to eat and finally agreed on the Marine Café because it was cheap and the cutest boy in class lived nearby.

Ten years later, the same girlfriends – now twenty-five – discussed where to meet for dinner. Finally they agreed to meet at the Marine Café because there was no cover charge, the beer was cheap, the band was good, and there were plenty of good-looking men.

Ten years later, the same girlfriends – now thirty-five – debated where to meet for dinner. Finally they decided to go to the Marine Café because it served good wine, it was near the gym and if they got there after eight there would be no children running around.

Ten years later, the same girlfriends – now forty-five – discussed where to meet for dinner. Finally they agreed on the Marine Café because the martinis were big and the waiters wore tight jeans.

Ten years later, the same girlfriends – now fifty-five – discussed where to meet for dinner. Finally they agreed on the Marine Café because the air-conditioning was efficient and the fish was good for their cholesterol.

Ten years later, the same girlfriends – now sixty-five – debated where to meet for dinner. Finally they decided on the Marine Café because they could get special rates if they went early, the lighting was good and the menu was in large print.

Ten years later, the same girlfriends – now seventy-five – discussed where to meet for dinner. Finally they agreed on the Marine Café because it had wheelchair access and the food wasn't too spicy.

Ten years later, the same girlfriends – now eighty-five – discussed where to meet for dinner. Finally they agreed on the Marine Café because they'd never been there before.

Special Offer

An elderly man and woman were sitting in the sunroom of a retirement home. After a while he whispered to her: 'For five pounds I'll have sex with you on that rocking chair over there. For ten pounds I'll have sex with you on that couch. And for twenty pounds I'll take you to my room, light some candles and give you a night of passion you'll never forget.'

The woman considered the proposition for a moment, then rummaged through her purse and produced a twenty-pound note.

'So,' he said, 'you want a night in my room?'

'No,' said the old woman, 'I want it four times in the rocker.'

Million-Dollar Question

A wife was beginning to feel insecure about her looks as she turned fifty. Seeking reassurance, she said to her husband: 'You wouldn't sleep with Angelina Jolie for a million dollars, would you?'

'Don't be ridiculous,' said the husband. 'Where am I going to raise a million dollars?'

Fear of the Dentist

For weeks an elderly man had been putting off making a dental appointment until finally he summoned the courage to phone the surgery.

'I'm sorry,' said the receptionist, 'but the dentist is out just now.'

'Oh, thank you,' said the old man, relieved. 'When will he be out again?'

Shopping Dash

A man received a phone call at work from his wife asking him to pick up some organic vegetables on his way home for that night's dinner. At the supermarket he searched everywhere for organic vegetables but, to his intense frustration, was unable to find any. Eventually he had to ask a young member of staff where they were.

'Organic vegetables?' said the store worker, scratching his head. 'What do you mean by organic?'

Exasperated, the husband explained: 'These vegetables are for my wife. Have they been sprayed with poisonous chemicals?'

'No, sir,' replied the store worker. 'You'll have to do that yourself.'

Service with a Smile

A businessman travelling through rural England decided to stop the night at a picturesque country inn, the George and Dragon. Checking in at reception, he asked the lady co-owner, a sturdy woman in her sixties, whether meals were still being served at the bar.

'No,' she replied bluntly. 'Last meals are 8p.m. sharp. It is now eight minutes past eight. You're too late.'

'Can't I even get a sandwich?' he asked sheepishly.

'No, not even a sandwich,' she insisted. 'The chef has packed up, and I'm certainly not going to start slaving away in the kitchen at this time of night just because you haven't planned your itinerary properly.'

'Very well,' he said resignedly. 'Is there any chance of having breakfast served in my room in the morning?'

'Certainly not,' she snapped. 'All breakfasts are served in the dining room at 7.30a.m. prompt, and if you're too lazy to get up in time, that's your lookout. Any more questions?'

'Yes,' replied the businessman. 'Do you think I might have a word with George?'

My Son is Gay!

Mrs Cohen and Mrs Rosenthal met for lunch. Mrs Cohen announced: 'I have good news and bad news.'

'Tell me the bad news first,' said Mrs Rosenthal. 'Get it over with.'

'Very well,' said Mrs Cohen, taking a deep breath. 'My son Michael phoned me last night and told me he is gay.'

'Never!' exclaimed Mrs Rosenthal. 'And after all that you've done for that boy! You've been such a wonderful mother. You mustn't blame yourself. So what's the good news?'

Mrs Cohen said: 'He's marrying a doctor!'

New Boots

An elderly couple were on holiday in London. Sam had always wanted a pair of cowboy boots so when he saw some on sale in a specialist shop he eagerly bought them and wore them back to the hotel.

He walked proudly into the room and said to his wife: 'Notice anything different, Peggy?'

She looked him up and down and said: 'No.'

'Come on, Peggy,' he pleaded. 'Take a good look. You must notice something different?'

'No.'

So Sam marched into the bathroom, undressed and walked back into the room completely naked except for his new boots. 'Now do you notice anything different?' he demanded.

Peggy replied calmly: 'What's different, Sam? It's hanging down today, it was hanging down yesterday and it'll be hanging down tomorrow.'

'The reason it's hanging down,' yelled Sam, 'is because it's pointing at my new boots!'

Peggy shook her head knowingly. 'You should've bought a hat, Sam, You should've bought a hat.'

Dirty Dancing

Farmer Jack was passing by Bob's hay barn one day when, peering through a gap in the door, he saw old Bob performing a slow striptease in front of a rusty red tractor.

After watching Bob gyrating sensually around the chassis and cab of the tractor for several minutes, shedding items of clothing as he went, Jack finally called out: 'What on earth are you doing?'

'You scared the life out of me!' exclaimed Bob, embarrassed. 'But if you must know, I'm following the doctor's orders. You see, my wife and I have been having a bit of trouble in the bedroom department lately, so the doctor said I should do something sexy to a tractor.'

Is it a Wig?

An elderly lady travelling on a bus tapped the shoulder of the woman sitting directly in front of her.

'Excuse me,' she said. 'I'm fascinated by your hair. Tell me, are you wearing a wig?'

'Yes, I am,' hissed the other passenger.

'Really? You'd never guess!'

Pigeon Fancier

An old lady liked to go to the park and feed the pigeons. She always had dozens of birds around her, flocking to eat the bread she had thrown on the ground.

Then one day a man appeared and told her off. He barked: 'You shouldn't be feeding the pigeons when there are thousands of people starving in Africa.'

'Sorry,' said the old lady, 'but with my arthritis I can't throw bread that far!'

Good Excuse

A young police officer pulled over an eighty-three-year-old woman driver for speeding.

'Madam,' he said, 'you were doing nearly twice the speed limit. Can you give me a good reason why I shouldn't book you?'

'Yes, officer,' she replied. 'You see, I had to get to my destination before I forgot where I was going!'

Large Family

A male census-taker rang the doorbell and was surprised when a middle-aged woman answered the door stark naked.

'Don't be alarmed,' she said. 'I'm a nudist.'

Although extremely embarrassed, the census-taker proceeded to ask his standard questions. 'How many children do you have?' he inquired.

'Nineteen,' she replied.

'Nineteen?!' he said. 'Madam, you're not a nudist – you just don't have time to get dressed!'

Home Truths

An elderly couple were competing in their golf club's annual seniors' tournament. On the final hole, the wife had to make a six-inch putt to tie with the leading score, but she missed and they lost out on their chance of victory.

In the car on the way home, the husband was still fuming about the miss. 'I can't believe you didn't hole that putt,' he snapped. 'It was no longer than my willy!'

'Yes, dear,' she replied. 'But it was much harder!'

Ulterior Motive

Two mature women were discussing their respective husbands. 'Ted and I just seem to fight all the time,' said one. 'In fact, I've been so upset that I've lost twelve pounds over the past three months.'

'Why don't you leave him?' asked her friend.

'Not yet. I want to lose another nine pounds first.'

Letter to God

A post office worker at the main sorting office found an unstamped, handwritten envelope addressed to God. He opened it and discovered it was from an elderly lady who was distressed because her life's savings – £200 – had been stolen. She was telling God that she would be cold and hungry at Christmas without divine intervention.

The postal worker was so moved by the old woman's plight that he organized a collection among his colleagues. They dug deep and donated £180, which they arranged to be delivered to her later that day by courier.

A week later, the same postal worker recognized the same handwriting on another envelope addressed to God and opened it. The letter read: 'Dear God, Thank you for the £180 for Christmas, which would have been so miserable otherwise.

'P.S. It was £20 short, but that was probably those thieving workers at the post office.'

Coach Trip

As a coach load of senior American tourists on a visit to England drove through Wiltshire, the guide pointed out various places of interest. When they approached Stonehenge, the guide announced: 'This is Stonehenge, a megalithic monument dating from about 2,800 BC. It consisted originally of thirty upright stones, their tops linked by lintel stones to form a continuous circle about a hundred feet across. The uprights were built from local sandstone, and each stone weighs around twenty-six tons.'

At the back of the coach, one tourist turned to his wife and said: 'Pretty impressive, huh?'

'Yes,' she agreed. 'But wouldn't you think they'd have built it further back from the main road?'

The Wrong House

An old man was dozing in his favourite chair one afternoon when he was awoken by the sound of the doorbell. He shuffled to the door and when he opened it, he saw a beautiful young woman standing there.

'Oh, I'm sorry,' she said. 'I'm at the wrong house.'

'Honey, you're at the right house,' the old man assured her, 'but you're fifty years too late!'

Late Night Call

A forgetful old lady climbed out of bed to answer the phone at two o'clock in the morning. The voice on the other end of the line said: 'Is that the Blue Ocean nightclub?'

'No, it isn't,' said the old lady. 'This is a private residence.'

'Oh, I must have the wrong number. Sorry to have troubled you.'

'It's no trouble,' said the old lady. 'I had to get up to answer the phone anyway.'

Gas Problem

An elderly couple were attending a church service. Halfway through the wife leaned over and whispered: 'I've just done a silent fart. What do you think I should do?'

Her husband said: 'Put a new battery in your hearing aid.'

Troubled Times

Three Jewish mothers met for lunch.

The first wailed: 'What a terrible week I've had! On Monday, my son's wife of fourteen years, the mother of my three grandchildren, suddenly announced that she's leaving him for another man! I may never get to see the little ones again.'

'You think you've got problems?' exclaimed the second. 'My son the lawyer has a terminal disease. He may only have weeks to live! I don't know how I'll cope.'

'That's nothing!' declared the third. 'My cleaning woman resigned yesterday!'

Always Complaining

A man asked a hospital doctor: 'Can you give me an update on the condition of my elderly aunt, Mrs Walters, who was admitted yesterday?'

'Ah yes, Mrs Walters,' sighed the doctor. 'In the short time she has been here, she has done nothing but complain. She has complained about her bed, she has complained about the food, she has complained about the other patients and she has complained about the nurses.'

The man frowned. 'So you mean–'

'Yes,' interrupted the doctor. 'I'm afraid she's critical.'

Sales Talk

Approaching a department store's fabric counter, a pretty young woman said to the salesman: 'I'd like this material for a dress. How much does it cost?'

'For a beautiful girl like you, just one kiss per metre,' smiled the smooth-talking salesman.

'OK' said the girl. 'I'll take ten metres.'

With anticipation written all over his face, the salesman quickly measured out the cloth, wrapped it and then teasingly held it out waiting for his reward. Instead the girl snatched the package, pointed to the wizened, toothless old man standing next to her and smiled: 'Grandpa here will pay the bill.'

Secret of Longevity

A 109-year-old man was asked by a local newspaper reporter for the secret of his longevity.

'It's hard to say,' said the old man, 'but I think the reason I have lived for so long is because I gave up sex.'

'When did you give up sex?' asked the reporter.

'Sixteen years ago.'

'I see,' said the reporter. 'And if it's not too personal a question why did you give up sex?'

'I had to. I like older women!'

Golf Cheat

Bert and Jack played a weekly game of golf in their old age until suddenly the arrangement stopped. 'Why don't you play golf with Jack any more?' asked Bert's wife.

Bert said: 'Would you play with someone who kicks his ball out of a bunker when no one is looking, who deliberately coughs halfway through his opponent's backswing and who lies about his handicap?'

'I guess not,' said the wife.

'Well, neither will Jack.'

Senior Moment

An old lady phoned hotel reception to complain that she was trapped in her room.

'I can't get out!' she said.

'Why not?' asked the receptionist. 'Have you tried the door?'

'Of course I have,' said the old lady. 'But there are only three doors in here. The first is the bathroom, the second is the wardrobe, and the third has a sign on it that says "Do Not Disturb".'

Wedding Photos

Two senior citizens got married. On their wedding night, the bride stepped out of the shower wrapped in a robe. Her new husband said: 'You don't have to be shy now – we're married.'

So she took off her robe to reveal her naked body.

'Let me take your picture,' said the husband.

'Why?' she asked, embarrassed.

'So I can carry your beauty next to my heart for the rest of my days.'

He took the photo and then went to have a shower himself. A few minutes later he emerged wrapped in a robe.

'Why are you wearing a robe?' she asked. 'Remember, you don't have to be shy now – we're married.'

So he removed his robe to reveal his naked body.

'Let me take your picture,' she said.

'Why?' he asked, grinning.

'So I can get it enlarged.'

Party Pooper

As they drove home from a party late one evening, a wife turned to her middle-aged husband and said: 'Have I ever told you how sexy and irresistible to women you are?'
'I don't believe you have, dear,' he replied, flattered.
'Then what in hell's name gave you that idea at the party?'

European Tour

A senior married couple were talking to a neighbour about their road trip to Europe.

'It sounds as if you had a wonderful time in Italy,' said the friend, 'but I didn't know you were planning to take in Spain as well.'

'We weren't,' said the wife, 'but Bill simply will not ask for directions.'

Covering His Embarrassment

A young man went for a swim in a lake but when he got there, he realized he had forgotten his swimming trunks. Since there was nobody about, he decided to jump in naked. After finishing his swim, he climbed out and was about to get dressed when he saw two old ladies approaching. He quickly grabbed a small bucket, held it over his privates and breathed a huge sigh of relief. But when the old ladies started to giggle, he began to feel a bit awkward.

One old lady said to him: 'I have a special gift. I can read minds – and I bet I can read yours.'

'Go on then,' said the young man dismissively. 'Tell me what I'm thinking.'

'Right now,' she said, 'I bet you think that the bucket you're holding has a bottom.'

Fear of Flying

An old lady was terrified of visiting her family in Australia because she was always afraid that there would be a bomb on board the plane. Her family tried to convince her that the risk was minimal and eventually persuaded her to consult an actuary.

'What are the chances of someone having a bomb on a plane?' she asked.

'Very small,' replied the actuary. 'About one in ten thousand.'

'And what are the chances of two people having a bomb on the same plane?'

'Even smaller,' said the actuary. 'Something like one in a billion. Virtually zero.'

After that, the old lady was happy to fly… so long as she always took a bomb on board with her.

Holding It In

A husband was standing on the bathroom scales, desperately holding his stomach in. Thinking that he was trying to reduce his weight, his wife commented: 'I don't think that will help.'

'It does,' he said. 'It's the only way I can read the numbers!'

Her Dream Present

Waking up on the eve of their golden wedding anniversary, a woman said to her husband: 'I just had a dream that you gave me the most beautiful twenty-four-carat-gold necklace. What do you think it means?'

'You'll know tomorrow,' he said with a smile.

She couldn't think about anything else for the rest of the day and was counting down the hours until the following morning. Finally morning came. As she sat up in bed on their anniversary, her husband handed her a beautifully wrapped small package.

She opened it excitedly to find a book titled *The Meaning of Dreams.*

Silent Treatment

Day after day an elderly hospital patient would put his ear to the wall and listen intently. The doctor observed this strange ritual but said nothing until one day his professional curiosity finally got the better of him. Intrigued as to what the patient might be listening to, the doctor decided to put his own ear to the wall, but heard nothing.
So he turned to the patient and said: 'I can't hear anything.'
'I know,' said the patient. 'It's been like that for months!'

Life Cycle

At age four success is…not peeing in your pants.

At age twelve success is…having friends.

At age seventeen success is…having a driver's licence.

At age twenty success is…having sex.

At age thirty-five success is…having money.

At age fifty success is…having money.

At age sixty-five success is…having sex.

At age seventy success is…having a driver's licence.

At age seventy-five success is…having friends.

At age eighty success is…not peeing in your pants.

Night Stalker

An elderly nun was walking home from the convent one night when a young man jumped out from behind some bushes and had his way with her. Afterwards, he was overcome with guilt and begged her not to tell anyone.

'I cannot keep this quiet,' she insisted. 'It would be wrong. I am duty bound to tell the Mother Superior.'

'And what will you tell her?' asked the young man.

'I will say that I was walking home from the convent when a young man jumped out of the bushes and had sex with me twice…unless you're tired.'

Grandma in Trouble

A young boy had been staying with his grandmother during the school holidays. He had been playing outside with his friends for an hour when he came into the house and said: 'Grandma, what is it called when two people are sleeping in the same room and one is on top of the other?'

She was taken aback by the question but decided to tell him the truth. 'It's called sexual intercourse, darling.'

'Oh, OK,' said the boy, and he ran back outside to play with the other kids.

A few minutes later he came back in and said angrily: 'Grandma, it's not called sexual intercourse! It's called bunk beds! And Billy's mother wants to talk to you!'

Nothing but the Best

A proud mother took her thirty-year-old son Isaac to meet her best friend.

'What do you do for a living?' asked the friend.

'I own some property,' replied Isaac modestly.

'Some property!' exclaimed his mother. 'He owns a chain of fast-rising retail stores.'

'And where do you live?' asked the friend.

'I've got an apartment in town,' said Isaac.

'An apartment!' cried his mother. 'He has a luxury penthouse in the most sought-after block in town.'

'And what's your ambition?' asked the friend.

'I'm hoping to expand,' said Isaac quietly.

'Expand!' his mother interrupted. 'He's planning to buy Wal-Mart!'

Just then Isaac sneezed loudly.

'Have you got a cold?' asked the friend.

'A cold!' shrieked his mother. 'Isaac's got pneumonia!'

Extra Charge

A balding man went into a barber's shop and asked how much it would be for a haircut.

'Thirty dollars,' said the barber.

'Thirty dollars!' exclaimed the man. 'That's crazy! I've hardly got any hair. How can it be that expensive?'

The barber explained: 'It's five dollars for the actual cut, and twenty-five dollars for the search fee.'

A Bump on the Head

After undergoing a particularly complicated operation, an elderly patient complained that he could feel some sort of bump on his head and that he had a pounding headache. As the operation had been on his stomach, these were not the type of side effects that the nurses had expected. Concerned that the patient might be suffering from post-operative shock, one of them mentioned the symptoms to the surgeon who had carried out the operation.

'Don't worry,' said the surgeon. 'It's not shock. He really does have a bump on his head. Halfway through the operation we ran out of anaesthetic.'

Those Were the Days

Three old ladies were sitting in their retirement home reminiscing. The first old lady recalled shopping at the greengrocer's, and demonstrated with her hands the length and thickness of a cucumber that she used to be able to buy for a penny.

The second old lady nodded, adding that onions were once much bigger and cheaper. She then used her hands to demonstrate the size of two big onions that she used to be able to buy for a penny each.

The third old lady remarked: 'I can't hear a word you're saying, but I remember the guy you're talking about.'

New Bath

An old man went into a hardware store
and asked to buy a bath.
'Would you like one with a plug?' said
the sales assistant.
The old man looked at him aghast and
said: 'Don't tell me they've gone electric!'

On the Prowl

A handsome middle-aged man was sitting at a bar when a woman accidentally spilled her drink over him. As he dried himself off, they started to chat. After a while she said: 'You look like my third husband.'

'Really?' he said. 'How many times have you been married?'

'Twice,' she replied.

Lunch Hitch

Two elderly men went into a bar one lunchtime and after some confusion ordered two beers. Looking lost, they then sat at a table, opened lunchboxes that their wives had prepared and started to eat.

Witnessing this, the waiter marched over to their table and told them: 'Sorry, but you can't eat your own sandwiches in here!'

The two men looked at each other bewildered, shrugged their shoulders, and exchanged sandwiches.

Where There's a Will

An old man called on his solicitor to make a will. 'What exactly do I have to do?' he asked.

'It's perfectly straightforward,' said the solicitor. 'Just answer a few questions then leave it all to me.'

The old man looked worried. 'I quite like you,' he said, 'but I was planning to leave some of it to my wife.'

Seeing Double

A census-taker in Mississippi went up to a trailer home and knocked on the door. When an old woman answered, he asked her the names and ages of her children.

'Let me see now,' said the old woman. 'There are the twins, Jimmy and Johnny, they're forty-six. And the twins, Jay and Kay, they're forty-five. And the twins, Charlie and Charlene, they're forty-four.'

'Hang on!' said the census-taker. 'Did you get twins every time?'

'Heck no,' answered the old woman. 'There were hundreds of times we didn't get nothing.'

A Sight to Behold

In her later years, a woman started to put on weight alarmingly and was advised by her doctor to go on a strict diet. But because she kept raiding the fridge she continued to pile on the pounds until one day she got her butt stuck on the toilet seat.

Her husband summoned the doctor but failed to explain what the problem was. Meanwhile the husband managed to remove the seat from the toilet bowl but it was still wedged fast to his wife's backside. He then suggested that she go and kneel on the bed until the doctor arrived.

When the doctor turned up, the husband showed him straight into the bedroom where the wife was kneeling with her back to the door.

'What do you think, doctor?' asked the husband.

'Very nice,' said the doctor, 'but why such a cheap frame?'

Hospital Horrors

An old man woke up in the recovery room following an operation and sighed: 'I'm so glad that's over.'

'You're lucky,' said the patient in the next bed. 'They left a scalpel inside me and had to cut me open again.'

'That's awful!' said the old man.

'They had to open me up again, too,' said the patient on the other side. 'They'd left a pair of surgical scissors inside me.'

'How terrible!' said the old man.

Just then, the surgeon who had operated on the old man poked his head around the door and asked: 'Has anybody seen my hat?'

The old man fainted.

Over the Border

An elderly gentleman living in a remote cottage in the country received a visit from a council official. 'I have to inform you,' said the official, 'that due to boundary changes your home is no longer in Scotland but in England.'

'Thank goodness for that,' said the old man. 'I don't think I could stand another of those Scottish winters.'

Death Notice

A woman phoned her local newspaper to ask if she could put a notice in the obituary column.

'Certainly, madam,' said the operator.

'How much do funeral notices cost?' asked the woman.

'Five dollars per word.'

'Good. Do you have a paper and pencil handy?'

'Yes, madam.'

'Write this then: "McHenry died."'

'Sorry, madam, I forget to tell you: there's a five word minimum.'

The woman thought for a moment and then said: 'OK. Got your pencil and paper?'

'Yes, madam.'

'Right. Print this: "McHenry died. Chevrolet for sale."'

Weighty Problem

A woman in her sixties took her grown-up daughter to one side and said: 'Darling, I don't want you to think I have diabetes because I'm fat. I have diabetes because it runs in our family.'

The daughter shook her head in despair. 'No, Mum,' she replied, 'you have diabetes because no one runs in our family.'

Retirement Gift

After forty-eight years of delivering mail to the same neighbourhood, it was Norm the mailman's last day at work. At the first house on his final round, the family formed a guard of honour and applauded him up the driveway. At the second house, he was given a box of cigars. At the third house, he was presented with a dozen bottles of his favourite beer. At the fourth house, he was greeted by a sprightly old lady who immediately dragged him upstairs, pinned him to the bed and had sex with him for nearly an hour. Then she led him exhausted back downstairs and cooked him the most sumptuous four-course breakfast. Norm's head was still spinning when he noticed a dollar bill tucked underneath his breakfast plate.

'Mrs Wilson, that was amazing,' he said, 'but what's with the dollar bill?'

The old lady explained: 'Last night I told my husband that today would be your final round and I suggested we should do something special for you. He said: "Screw him! Give him a dollar." The breakfast was my idea.'

Crossed Wires

Two old farmers were standing in a field. One said: 'Have you seen my flock of cows?'

The other corrected him: 'Herd of cows.'

'Of course I've heard of cows,' said the first. 'I've got a whole flock of them!'

Plastered

Arriving home drunk late one night, a husband cut himself when he accidentally walked into a shelf in the hallway. With blood trickling down his face, he went straight upstairs to the bathroom to repair the wounds.

The next morning his wife said: 'You came home drunk last night, didn't you?'

'No,' he replied, lying through his teeth.

'Then perhaps you can explain to me why there are plasters all over the bathroom mirror?'

The Dentist's Chair

A senior man went to the dentist to get a tooth pulled.

'I'll give you an injection to numb your mouth,' said the dentist.

'No, please don't,' said the patient. 'I'm afraid of needles.'

'Right. In which case I'll give you a gas anaesthetic to put you to sleep.'

'No,' said the patient. 'I'm allergic to gas.'

So the dentist searched his medicine cabinet for something suitable. Eventually he found a packet of pills and said: 'Here, take two of these.'

'What are they?' asked the patient.

'Viagra.'

'Viagra?! Why on earth are you giving me Viagra?'

'Well,' said the dentist, 'although they won't help numb the pain, they will give you something to hang on to while I pull your tooth.'

Health Care

An elderly woman with expensive private health care received a call from the doctor's receptionist.

'Mrs McKenzie?' said the receptionist. 'You know the treatment you had recently for your rheumatism? Well, I'm sorry to have to tell you but your cheque came back.'

'That's OK,' said the woman. 'So did my rheumatism.'

One Man and His Moped

A young man was taking his new car out for a spin. As he stopped at traffic lights, an old man on a moped drew up alongside and cast an admiring glance at the shiny car.

'Nice car, son,' said the old man. 'Do you mind if I take a quick look inside?'

'Sure,' said the driver. So the old man poked his head through the car window and looked around. Then leaning back on his moped, he confirmed: 'That's a real nice car.'

Just then the traffic lights changed and the young driver decided to show the old man just what his new car was capable of. So he put his foot down and roared off at 80mph.

A few seconds later, he noticed a dot in his rear-view mirror that quickly got closer. Suddenly it ploughed into the back of his car. He jumped out and found the old man and his moped lying in the road.

'I can see you're badly hurt,' he said to the old man. 'Is

there anything I can do?'

'Yeah,' replied the old man, 'unhook my braces from your side-view mirror!'

A Bitter Divorce

Having been granted a divorce on the grounds of her husband's adultery, a woman was forced to move out of the house she had lovingly tended for thirty-eight years. She spent two whole days packing her belongings into boxes, crates and suitcases before on the third day the removal men came to collect her things. That evening, she sat alone in the house for the last time, preparing herself a final farewell meal of prawns and caviar, which she ate by candlelight at their beautiful dining room table. She was sad but bitter, too, and at the end of her meal she went into every room and placed a few half-eaten prawn shells dipped in caviar into the hollows of the curtain rods. She then tidied up the kitchen and left.

When the husband moved back in with his new young partner, everything was fine for the first few days. Then slowly the house began to acquire a strange smell, which, despite endless scouring and mopping, would not disappear. Vents were checked for dead rodents and carpets were steam cleaned. Air fresheners were hung everywhere. Pest exterminators were called in to set off gas canisters, which, made such a mess the couple had to move out for a few days and replace all their expensive wool carpets. But still nothing worked. After a while, friends stopped coming to visit, repairmen refused to work in the house and the maid quit, fearing for her health.

Eventually they could bear the stench no longer and decided to put the house up for sale. But prospective buyers were immediately put off by the smell and, despite the price being greatly reduced, several months later they had still not managed to sell it. Things were so bad that they had to borrow a vast sum of money from the bank in order to purchase a new home.

Word of their misfortune reached the ears of his ex-wife, who called to ask him how things were going. When he relayed the saga of the rotting house, she listened politely and said that she missed her old home terribly. She suggested that she would even be willing to reduce her divorce settlement in exchange for getting her beloved house back.

The husband almost bit off her hand and made sure that the paperwork for the transaction was rushed through before she had a chance to change her mind. With everything signed and sealed, he and his girlfriend congratulated themselves on finally finding a fool happy to take the horrible, stinking house off their hands and they smiled smugly as they watched the removal company pack up everything to take to their new home.

And just to spite his ex-wife, they even took the curtain rods!

Flying Visit

An old lady went to the hospital outpatients' department and said to a nurse: 'A wasp has given me a nasty sting. Is there something you can give me?'
'Whereabouts is it?' asked the nurse.
'I don't know,' said the old lady. 'It will be miles away by now!'

Earning Her Keep

A couple were admiring their large garden from the kitchen window. The wife said: 'Darling, sooner or later, we're going to have to make a proper scarecrow to keep the birds off the flower beds.'

'What's wrong with the one we've got?' asked the husband.

'Nothing, I suppose. But mother's arms are starting to get tired.'

Name That Tattoo

A woman went into a tattoo parlour and asked the artist to tattoo a picture of Johnny Depp on her right upper thigh and Brad Pitt on her left upper thigh. The artist obeyed her instructions, and when he had finished he handed her a mirror so she could inspect the work.

She looked at the right thigh and said: 'Hey! That's definitely Johnny Depp. Just look at those eyes.' Then she examined her left thigh but complained: 'That doesn't look anything like Brad Pitt.'

The artist disagreed and suggested they settle the argument by seeking the opinion of an impartial judge. So they went to the bar next door and asked an elderly man to identify the tattoos. The woman raised her skirt and dropped her panties, and the old man put his face up close. 'Well, ma'am,' he concluded, 'the one on your right thigh is definitely Johnny Depp. You can tell by the eyes and the cheek bones. The one on your left I'm not sure about – but the one in the middle is definitely Willie Nelson.'

Miaow!

Two middle-aged women were chatting in a coffee shop. 'Audrey, I know life can be tough,' said the first, 'but whenever I'm down in the dumps I buy myself a dress.'

'Really, Cynthia?' said the friend, eyeing her up and down. 'I've always wondered where you got them.'

Kicking up a Stink

While serving tea in the lounge of a retirement home, the nurse caught a whiff of something unpleasant. 'Right,' she said. 'Who's messed in their pants?'

Nobody answered, so she patrolled the room in a bid to trace the origin of the smell. Finally she found the culprit – an old man sitting in the corner.

'Why didn't you answer when I asked who had messed in their pants?' she said.

'Sorry,' said the old man. 'I thought you meant today.'

Only Trying to Help

Driving along a busy highway in winter, a little old lady pulled her car alongside a truck and shouted: 'Driver, you're losing your load!'

'I know,' yelled the truck driver. 'Mind your own business!' And he carried on driving.

Two miles further down the road, the old lady again drew alongside the truck and yelled across to the driver: 'You're definitely losing your load!'

'Go away!' shouted the truck driver impatiently.

Two miles further on, the old lady pulled alongside the truck once more and shouted: 'Driver, you really are losing your load!'

'For the last time, get lost!' yelled the truck driver. 'I'm gritting!'

Medical Advice

A woman rushed into a doctor's surgery and gasped: 'Doctor, my husband was asleep with his mouth open and he's swallowed a mouse! What shall I do?'

'Don't panic,' said the doctor reassuringly. 'All you need to do is tie a lump of cheese to a piece of string and lower it into your husband's mouth. As soon as the mouse takes a bite, haul it out.'

'Thank you so much, doctor,' said the woman, relieved. 'I'll go around to the fishmonger straight away and get a cod's head.'

'What do you want a cod's head for?' asked the doctor.

'Oh, I forgot to tell you,' said the woman. 'I've got to get the cat out first!'

Tight Fit

An elderly man entered a shoe shop and asked for a pair of brown shoes, size seven.

The sales assistant said: 'Are you sure, sir? You look like a size eleven to me.'

'Just bring me a size seven,' barked the old man.

So the assistant fetched a pair of size seven shoes, and the old man squeezed his feet into them with obvious discomfort. He then stood up in the shoes, but it was clear he was in considerable pain.

'Are you absolutely sure you want these shoes?' repeated the assistant.

'Listen, sonny,' said the old man, 'my business of forty-eight years has just gone bust, I haven't seen my son since

1991 and my wife's run off with my best friend. The only pleasure I have left is to come home at night and take my shoes off!'

Technical Hitch

A middle-aged woman went to visit a friend in hospital. She hadn't been inside a hospital for over twenty years and felt very ignorant about all the new technology. A technician followed her into the elevator, wheeling a large, intimidating-looking machine with numerous tubes, wires and dials.

She looked at it and smiled: 'I certainly wouldn't want to be hooked up to that!'

'Neither would I,' replied the technician. 'It's a floor-cleaning machine.'

Yoga for Beginners

An old man went to his local gym to ask about yoga classes for beginners.
The instructor asked him: 'How flexible are you?'
The old man replied: 'I can't do Thursdays.'

Water Torture

Suffering from severe indigestion, an old man was advised by his doctor to drink warm water one hour before breakfast. However after three weeks there was no improvement in his condition – in fact, when he went back to the doctor, he complained that he was actually feeling worse than ever.

The doctor said: 'Did you drink warm water an hour before breakfast each day?'

'I tried,' replied the old man. 'But all I could manage was twenty minutes.'

Get it Right!

After thirty years of marriage, a man said to his wife: 'You know, we would have less arguments if you weren't so damn pedantic.'

She said: 'Fewer arguments...'

Everything Looks Great

My face in the mirror isn't wrinkled or drawn.
My house isn't dirty. The cobwebs are gone.
My garden looks lovely and so does my lawn.
I think I might never put my glasses back on.

Cheap Fix

A man in his sixties had become increasingly hard of hearing, so reluctantly he accepted that he needed to buy a hearing aid. However because money was tight he wanted the cheapest model on the market.

'How much do they cost?' he asked the sales assistant.

'Anything from £1.50 to £500.'

'Can I see the £1.50 model?' asked the man.

The sales assistant opened a box, placed the device around the customer's neck, and said: 'You just stick this button in your ear and run this length of string down to your pocket.'

'It's not very discreet,' said the man. 'How does it work?'

'For £1.50, it doesn't work,' said the sales assistant. 'But when people see it on you, they'll talk louder!'

Senior Slang

Senior citizens love to text and they even have their own vocabulary:

BYOW:
Bring Your Own Wheelchair

CBHI:
Covered by Health Insurance

FWP:
Friend With Pacemaker

JFO:
Just Fell Over

LMWO:
Laughing My Wig Off

MDPBD:
Must Dash, Pacemaker Battery Died

Remember, Remember

Two old friends were talking and one said to the other:
'Did you know that the second thing to go is your
memory?'

'What's the first?' his friend asked.

'I can't remember,' came the response.

Aches and Pains

The day after visiting a funfair, a middle-aged housewife
was in such agony she could barely walk.

'You know you're past your prime,' she said, 'when you
hurt all over and all you rode was the carousel.'

The Joys of Retirement

Retirement is the best thing that has happened to Bob. 'I never know what day of the week it is,' he gloated. 'All I know is, the day the big paper comes, I have to put on my suit and go to church.'

Clicking into Place

At his sixtieth birthday dinner a husband turned proudly to his wife and proclaimed: 'Everything's starting to click for me! My knees, my elbows, my neck …'

Wrinkle Cream

A middle-aged woman was busy getting ready for work when her nine-year-old daughter walked in and asked:

'Mum, what are you doing?'

'Putting on my wrinkle cream,' her mother answered.

'Oh,' came the response. 'I thought they were natural.'

Generation Gap

A ten-year-old girl had been set a class assignment to interview an old person about their life. She approached her aging uncle and asked him: 'What was the biggest historical event that happened during your childhood?'

'I'd have to say the moon walk,' her doting uncle replied.

'Was that dance really so important to you?' came the incredulous response.

Old-Timer

After working for months to get in shape, a middle-aged couple hiked to the bottom of the Grand Canyon and back. To celebrate their achievement they each bought an 'I hiked the canyon' T-shirt.

Not long after, the husband was wearing his T-shirt when he was approached by a young man.

'Did you really hike the canyon?' the young man asked.

Beaming with pride, the husband answered, 'Sure did!'

'No kidding!' the fellow said. 'What year?'

Trouble Speaking

A middle-aged woman was struck down with laryngitis and finally decided to go to the doctor. When she arrived at the surgery the nurse called her in and asked for her age. 'Forty-nine,' she whispered in response. 'Don't worry,' the nurse whispered back. 'I won't tell anyone.'

Getting Older

After celebrating her fiftieth birthday, a housewife went to get her driver's licence renewed. On arrival she was confronted by a matter-of-fact official who quickly tested her vision, took her photo and handed her the licence with the picture on it.

'You mean I have to look at this for the next ten years?' the housewife jokingly asked.

'Don't worry about it,' the official replied. 'In ten years it'll look good to you.'

Hard of Hearing

An old man decided his old wife was getting hard of hearing so he called the doctor to have her checked out. With no appointments available for another two weeks, the doctor suggested the old man carry out a simple test to check the extent of his wife's problem.

The doctor said: 'Stand about forty feet away from your wife and ask her a question in a normal conversational tone and see if she hears you. If not, go to thirty feet, then twenty feet, and so on until you get a response.'

So that evening while his wife was in the kitchen

cooking dinner, the old man stood forty feet away in the living room and said: 'Honey, what's for supper?'

No response.

So he edged closer in until he was roughly thirty feet away and said: 'Honey, what's for supper?'

No response.

He moved even closer so he was about twenty feet away. 'Honey, what's for supper?'

No response.

He moved into the kitchen, only ten feet away from his wife. 'Honey, what's for supper?'

Still no response.

So he walked right up behind her and repeated: 'Honey, what's for supper?'

His wife replied: 'For the fifth time, CHICKEN!'

No Place Like Home

A young chap happened upon an old man sobbing on a park bench. 'What's the matter?' the young man asked.

'I have a twenty-two-year-old wife at home. She rubs my back every morning and then gets up and makes me a cooked breakfast with fresh fruit and coffee.'

'Well, then why are you crying?' the young man asked.

'She makes me home-made soup for lunch followed by my favorite muffins. Then she cleans the house and then watches sport on TV with me for the rest of the afternoon.

'Well, why are you crying?' the young man repeated.

'For dinner she makes me a gourmet meal with wine and my favourite dessert, and then she makes love to me until the early hours.'

'Well, why in the world would you be crying?' the young man asked.

'I can't remember where I live!'

Ice Cream

An elderly husband and wife were both having problems remembering things. During a check-up, the doctor told them that they might want to start writing things down to help prompt their memories.

Later that night, while watching TV, the old man got up from his chair. 'Want anything while I'm in the kitchen?' he asked.

'Will you get me a bowl of ice cream?'

'Sure.'

'Don't you think you should write it down so you can remember it?' she prompted.

'No, I'll remember it,' he replied.

'Well, I'd like some chocolate drops on top, too. Maybe you should write it down. I don't want you to forget.'

'Don't worry, I'll remember. You want a bowl of ice cream with chocolate drops.'

'I'd also like whipped cream. I'm certain you'll forget that. Please write it down.' she urged.

Irritated, he said: 'I don't need to write it down, I'll remember! Ice cream with chocolate drops and whipped cream – I got it.'

He walked into the kitchen and returned twenty minutes later and handed his wife a plate of bacon and eggs. She stared at the plate for a moment and said: 'Where's my toast?'

Two Questions

A seventy-year-old man was deeply in love with his twenty-one-year-old lover. Getting down on one knee, he told her there were two things he'd like to ask her.

'Will you marry me?' came the first question.

'Yes, I'd be delighted to,' she replied. 'What else did you want to ask?'

'Will you help me up?'

Engagement Party

Two elderly men attended an engagement party. One of the men was dismayed to hear the bride-to-be had been living with her fiance for the past three years.

'All these people sleeping together before they're married,' he lamented. 'I didn't sleep with my wife before we were married. Did you?'

'I don't know,' answered the other man, thoughtfully. 'What was her maiden name?'

No Reservation

An elderly man and his wife arrived at a restaurant only to be told there was a forty-five-minute wait for a table.

'Young man, we're both ninety years old,' the gentleman informed the maître d'. 'We may not have forty-five minutes left.'

Old in Some Ways

During lessons a teacher was asked by one of the children: 'How old are you, Miss?'

'You shouldn't really ask an adult's age,' the teacher replied, 'but I'll tell you if you promise to keep it a secret. I'm fifty.'

'Wow, you don't look that old,' the boy said.

'Parts of her do,' chipped in another child.

Emergency Services

A middle-aged housewife called an ambulance as she was having difficulty breathing. The paramedic rushed to her home and immediately attached a sensor to her finger to check her pulse. Gathering as much information as possible, the paramedic asked: 'How old are you, madam?'

'Fifty-eight,' the invalid replied. 'What does that do?' she asked, nodding at the device on her finger.

'It's a lie detector,' replied the paramedic. 'What did you say your age was again?'

'Sixty-seven,' she confessed.

Forgotten Pleasures

Two elderly gentlemen were sitting in rocking chairs outside their nursing home when a pretty young woman walked by.

'Did you see her?' one of the gentlemen asked the other.

'Sure did. She was lovely, wasn't she?' he replied.

'She sure was. I'd like to take her out for a drink and some dinner and…and…what was that other thing we used to do?'

Bad Memory

An old man visited the doctor. After an extensive medical examination, the doctor said: 'I have good news and bad news for you. Do you want the good news or the bad news first?'

The old man was concerned and asked for the bad news first.

The doctor said: 'I'm sorry to say that you have cancer and you have only about two years to live.'

The old man was shocked. 'So what's the good news?' he asked.

The doctor said: 'You also have Alzheimer's and in approximately three months you will have forgotten everything I have told you.'

Birthday Boy

Three mischievous old ladies were sitting on a bench outside a nursing home when an old man shuffled past.

They yelled to him: 'We bet we can tell exactly how old you are!'

'Impossible!' the old man scoffed.

'Sure we can,' said one of the women. 'Just drop your pants and we'll tell you your exact age.'

So the old man took off his clothes.

'Now spin around three times,' they commanded.

Reluctantly the old man spun around three times and nearly toppled over because it made him so giddy.

When he had finished, the women called out: 'You're eighty-eight years old.'

Standing with his pants around his ankles, the old man said: 'That's right. How in the world did you work that out?'

The women cackled.

'We were at your birthday party yesterday!'

Can't Remember...

Wendy was extremely proud of her first baby, so when her mother came to stay she suggested that she might like to see the baby have its bath. Afterwards Wendy asked her mother what she thought of the baby.

'Oh, it's a lovely baby,' said the mother, 'but tell me: is it a boy or a girl?'

'Have you lost your glasses?' laughed Wendy.

'No, dear,' replied the mother, 'but I have lost my memory.'

Memory Like a Sieve

A man collecting in a shopping mall asked a woman for a donation to an Alzheimer's charity.

'But I already gave to you just now,' she said. 'Don't you remember?'

Pick Pocket

An absent-minded man arrived home from
work to find that someone had stolen
his wallet.
'How did that happen?' demanded his wife.
'How come you didn't feel a hand in
your pocket?'
'I did,' replied the man, 'but I thought it
was mine.'

Empty Seat

After a twenty-five-minute bus journey, Betty arrived at her daughter's house looking tired and agitated.

'Are you all right, Mother?' asked her daughter.

'Not really, dear,' said Betty. 'I feel a little nauseous from sitting backwards on the bus.'

'Oh, you poor thing. Why didn't you ask the person opposite you to swap seats?'

'I couldn't,' said Betty. 'That seat was empty.'

Two Coats

On a warm summer's day, a woman was surprised to see her neighbour painting his garden shed while wearing a raincoat over a thick woollen jacket.

'Aren't you hot?' she called out.

'Yes, I am a bit,' he replied breathlessly.

'Then why are you wearing all those clothes on a day like this?'

'Because,' he answered, 'it says here on the tin: "For best results, put on two coats".'

Who Am I?

An elderly man called in to a bank to apply for a new savings account.

The clerk fetched the appropriate form from the drawer of a filing cabinet and said: 'Could you tell me your age, please, sir?'

The old man looked blank for a while and muttered: 'I'm sorry, I've completely forgotten. But it'll come to me if you give me a minute or two.'

He then started counting on his fingers and eventually came up with a triumphant 'Eighty-one!'

'Thanks,' said the clerk. 'And could I have your name, please?'

Again the old man looked baffled but then he started singing quietly to himself, his head bobbing from side to side for about fifteen seconds. Finally he replied: 'Ah, there it is: Bert. Bert Brown.'

By now the clerk was totally mystified by the old man's memory aids and asked: 'I hope you don't mind me asking, sir, but what were you doing when I asked you your name? You appeared to be singing to yourself.'

'I was!' replied the old man. 'I was just running through that song: "Happy birthday to you, happy birthday to you, happy birthday dear…"'

Sleep Easy

An elderly woman went into the doctor's surgery. When the doctor asked why she was there, she replied: 'I'd like to have some birth-control pills.'

Taken aback, the doctor thought for a minute and then said: 'Excuse me, but you're seventy-five years old. What use could you have for birth-control pills?'

The woman responded: 'They help me sleep better.'

The doctor thought some more. 'How on earth do birth-control pills help you to sleep?'

The woman answered: 'I put them in my granddaughter's orange juice and I sleep better at night.'

The Confession

A middle-aged man walked into a Catholic church, sat down in the confessional box and said nothing. The bewildered priest coughed to attract his attention, but still the man said nothing. The priest then knocked on the wall three times in a final attempt to get the man to speak. Finally, the man replied: 'No use knocking, mate – there's no paper in this one either.'

The New Phone

Wanting to buy his elderly mother something useful for her seventy-fifth birthday, Jonathan bought her a mobile phone. After he had explained to her all the features on the phone, she was absolutely delighted with the gift.

The next day she was out shopping when her phone rang. 'Hi, Mom,' said Jonathan. 'How do you like your new phone?'

'I love it,' she replied. 'It's so compact and neat, and your voice is as clear as a bell. And I love all the different features. Isn't technology marvellous? There's just one thing I don't understand though.'

'What's that, Mom?'

'How did you know I was at the supermarket?'

Absent Friend

Old Arnold was shuffling in his slippers along the hallway of a retirement home as if he was driving a car.

'What are you doing, Arnold?' asked an orderly.

'I'm driving to Chicago,' replied Arnold.

The orderly smiled to himself and then went to check George's room. He was surprised to find George pleasuring himself.

'What are you doing, George?' asked the orderly.

George said: 'I'm having my way with Arnold's wife while he's in Chicago!'

A Good Moan

A newlywed senior couple were in bed in a hotel room on their first night. She was just lying there motionless and he was struggling to get aroused. Eventually he said to her: 'This is no good; you'll have to do something.'

'Like what?' she asked.

'Oh, you know,' he said. 'Moaning and stuff.'

So they started again and she said: 'Look at the state of those curtains. Have you seen the dust on that table? And you haven't folded your trousers properly…'

Home Cooking

A woman who was an enthusiastic – but not always accomplished – cook loved to try out new recipes on her long-suffering husband. One morning she served him some home-made cinnamon rolls for breakfast and waited eagerly for his reaction. When none was immediately forthcoming, she said: 'If I baked these commercially, how much do you think I could get for one of them?'

Without looking up from his newspaper, he replied: 'About ten years.'

Hard Times

A once wealthy middle-aged couple were faced with the prospect of having to make serious cutbacks. The husband said to his wife: 'If you were to learn how to cook and iron, my darling, we could do without the maid.'

To which the wife replied: 'And if you were to learn how to make love to me properly, we could do without the gardener!'

Blind Faith

An old man who was blind visited a brothel. Seeing his white stick, the brothel owner thought she would take advantage of the situation by pairing him with the roughest woman on the books, the one her other clients never chose.

So the pair went upstairs and the woman undressed, but when he started to run his hands over her spotty butt, he recoiled in horror.

'Don't worry,' she said. 'It's just a touch of acne.'

'Thank God!' said the blind man. 'I thought it was the price list!'

A Lack of Willpower

A middle-aged woman at a diet club sadly confessed that she had put on weight since the last gathering. 'I made my family's favourite chocolate cake at the weekend,' she told the group, 'and they ate half of it at dinner. The next day, I kept staring at the other half until I finally weakened and cut myself a thin slice. Well, I'm ashamed to say that once I got the taste there was no stopping me. One slice led to another and soon the whole cake was gone. I was totally dismayed by my lack of willpower, and I knew that my husband would be bitterly disappointed in me.'

'What did he say when he found out?' asked the group leader sympathetically.

'Oh, he never found out,' said the woman. 'I made another cake and ate half!'

Take Me Home

Two police officers saw an old woman staggering along the street. They stopped their patrol car and told her that she had had too much to drink. Instead of taking her to jail they decided to take her home. They loaded her into the police car with one officer driving and the other sitting in the back seat with the drunken woman. They drove around the streets and kept asking her where she lived but all she would say was, 'You're passionate', while stroking the officer's arm.

After getting the same response, 'You're passionate,' for the umpteenth time, they stopped the car and said to the old woman: 'Look, we have been driving around this city for over two hours and still you haven't told us where you live.'

The old woman replied: 'I keep trying to tell you, you're passing it!'

Short-Sighted Wife

An elderly man arrived home from the pub to find his wife in bed crying.

'What's the matter, darling?' he asked.

'We've had a burglar,' she sobbed.

'Did he get anything?' asked the husband.

'Too right he did!' she wailed. 'I thought it was you home early!'

A Close Shave

A senior citizen went into a barber's shop for a shave. He said to the barber: 'I never seem to be able to get a close shave around the cheeks. Do you have any ideas?'

'As a matter of fact I do,' replied the barber. Taking a small wooden ball from a drawer, he said: 'Place this between your cheek and gum.' So the customer put the ball in his mouth and experienced the closest shave ever. But after a minute or so, he spluttered: 'What happens if I swallow it?'

'No problem, sir. Just bring it back tomorrow like everyone else does.'